INTRODUCTION
TO RESEARCH METHODS
AND REPORT WRITING

*A Practical Guide for Students and Researchers
in Social Sciences and the Humanities*

By
Elia Shabani Mligo

RESOURCE *Publications* · Eugene, Oregon

INTRODUCTION TO RESEARCH METHODS AND REPORT WRITING
A Practical Guide for Students and Researchers in Social Sciences
and the Humanities

Resource Publications
An Imprint of Wipf and Stock Publishers
199 W. 8th Ave., Suite 3
Eugene, OR 97401

www.wipfandstock.com

PAPERBACK ISBN 13: 978-1-4982-7850-8
HARDCOVER ISBN 13: 978-1-4982-7852-2

Manufactured in the U.S.A.   04/05/2016

To my students of the course
on "Introduction to Research Methods"
I taught over the years for their thoughtful ideas
and patient spirit to learn

CONTENTS

PREFACE

WHY, IN THE FIRST PLACE, write an introductory book on research methods and report writing for students and researchers while there are large volumes of books on research in almost every field of study? Why write a book on research methods and report writing for students and researchers while there are plenty of research related materials already available in the internet? Students and researchers can access such materials from the internet and read them for free. They can download and use them at the time and place of their convenience. Why on earth endeavor towards a book on which many materials are resurgent, probably more interesting than the ones presented in this book, and can be accessed by students and researchers just for free?

There can be diverse answers to the questions stated above. While materials in most research books and internet sources may be results of authors' own creativity and thinking, this book comes directly from the classroom. It originates from students' own initiatives and thinking. After teaching the course on "Introduction to Research Methods" to undergraduate and non–degree students for some years, and witnessing the problems facing such students to understand, conduct, and report their research outcomes, I saw the necessity to address these needs. Pergiorgio Corbetta states this concern thus: "One of the problems facing a teacher of social research methodology is the shortage of manuals of a general, introductory nature."[1] As Corbetta saw, I also saw it necessary to provide teachers and students with a more simplified introductory book as a starting point in their teaching and research ventures before they could read the large volumes produced by research theorists. Therefore, this book is necessary

---

1. Corbetta, *Social Research*, 1.

to introduce teachers, students, and research beginners towards venturing into research projects in both non-degree and undergraduate courses. Moreover, the book can also be helpful to advanced researchers, those pursuing Masters degrees, Doctoral degrees, and professional researchers to guide them in their research and report writing works.

In order to accomplish this introductory role, the book provides the following helpful features: a definition of every main concept of the chapter before engaging the reader into the more details of it, a simple language to explain complex ideas used in research, and important pedagogical features (e.g., further reading list in every end of the chapter, appropriate examples where necessary, and a comprehensive reference list and appendices of important research aspects at the end of the book) in order to enable students and researchers explore further about issues discussed in subsequent chapters. Frankly speaking, this *Introduction to Research Methods and Report Writing* is an exciting, enriching, and rigorous book! Sincerely, it will be of help to both novices and experienced researchers in providing them a foundation for their own research ventures.

I appreciate the contribution of many people towards the production of this introductory book—students who attended my Introduction to Research Methods course over the years of my teaching at the University of Iringa–Amani Centre and at Tumaini University Makumira–Mbeya Centre—because they taught me greatly how to value the needs of the lowly. I also appreciate the contributions of my fellow lecturers and researchers at the University of Iringa and Tumaini University Makumira for their comments and suggestions, the librarians at the University of Oslo in Norway where I spent the first two weeks of February 2015 searching for ideas from other authors in order to ground mine, and Dr. Halvor Moxnes, Professor emeritus at the Faculty of Theology of the University of Oslo, for hosting me at his apartment during my search for literatures at the university library. The contributions of the above-mentioned people created to me conducive atmosphere to think and re-think about the importance of research to me as scholar and to students all over the world. I dedicate this book to my delighted students for teaching me research throughout the years I taught the course.

Elia Shabani Mligo (PhD)
Tumani University Makumira, Mbeya Teaching Center
Mbeya, Tanzania
October 2015

Chapter 1

MEANING AND IMPORTANCE OF RESEARCH

"In virtually every subject area, our knowledge is incomplete and problems are waiting to be solved. We can address our incomplete knowledge and unsolved problems by asking relevant questions and then seeking answers through systematic research. We have many tools at our disposal to help us do these things—not only physical tools but also mental and social tools."

—Leedy & Ormrod, *Practical Research*, 1)

INTRODUCTION

WE LIVE IN A WORLD WHERE THERE are more questions than answers. We ask questions to almost everything around us. Some of the questions we ask are the following:

a) Why do people die due to Malaria?

b) Why are African people and nations poor?

c) Why do we go to school?

d) How can we improve the living conditions of people in villages?

e) Which is the best way to use in order to be good academicians?

1

f) What is technology?

g) What problems are brought by the use of telephones in schools?

h) What do people in villages know about computers?

Every question above inquires about a particular situation in the community which needs some sort of improvement. This means that people are not always without a need. People are always in need of better life, in need of knowledge, in need of good relationship, in need of good shelter, in need of advancement in technology, in need of knowledge of what goes on in other places, and in need of communication. Therefore, need is prerequisite and inherent to human life and well being.

In order to satisfy people's needs, research is required. People's needs raise in them curiosity, puzzle, wonder, and surprise about the existence of problems around them that ultimately push them towards an urge to know.[1] In order to know why people die of malaria, why African people and states are poor, why there is a need to go to school, how we can improve the living conditions of people in villages, the best way to use in order to become good academicians, the meaning of technology, the problems caused by students' use of telephones in schools, and what people in villages know about computers, research must be done. Hence, this chapter introduces the meaning, basic types, assumptions, characteristics, importance of research, and the research process. The aim of this chapter is to provide students and researchers with the basic ideas of research in order for them to understand the discussion in the following chapters.

WHAT IS RESEARCH?

The most convenient and simple way to understand the concept of "research" is to deduce it from its etymology. Etymologically, the word research literally comes from two syllabi: the prefix "*Re–*" which means *again, once more, or anew,* and the verb "*–search*" which means *examine carefully, or test carefully.* We can say briefly that research is "*examining an issue again and carefully*" through asking relevant questions about it in search for answers.[2] We say that research is "examining an issue again" because the first examination was done when you encountered it for the first time; an encounter that caused you to have curiosity, puzzle, and wonder about it.

1. White, *Developing Research Questions*, 5.

2. Upgade & Shede, *Research Methodology*, 2.

In that sense, all human beings with a sound mind are researchers because they all wonder, are puzzled or surprised by their existing situations, and ask questions about those situations seeking answers for them.

Research can be formal or informal. There is a difference between informal (lay) research and formal (specialized) research. Formal research follows scientific procedures to discover answers about a problem, while informal research follows no scientific procedures.[3] However, our concern in this book is formal research; and whenever we mention the term 'research', it will refer to formal research.

There are several other advanced definitions of research, especially formal research. Some of these definitions are the following: first, research is the systematic search for knowledge about existing phenomena which are unknown to us. When we do not know about what causes malaria, we do research in order to learn about it. When we do not know why African people and states are poor, we do research in order to discern the reasons for the African poverty. When we do not know why people in villages have bad living conditions, we do research in order to know the reasons for their bad living conditions. Therefore, research is the systematic search for knowledge about things we do not know in order for us to know them.

Second, research is the search for answers about questions of our everyday life. Most of the questions above concern our everyday life. For an academician, there is no simplistic answer to any single question. Every question needs concrete answers that convince a person to whom it is provided. In order to have convincing answers for the question, one has to do research. This is why we say that research is the search for convincing (not satisfactory) answers to questions of our everyday life. Therefore, in doing research for answering the question we do three things: first, we pose the question itself (we determine the problem); second, we collect data in order to answer that question (we conduct research); third, we present the answer we have obtained from the collected data (we write a formal report to disseminate the findings).[4] These three things are important for any research done within the social sciences and the humanities; and they summarize what it really means by "social research."

Third, Nancy J. Vyhmeister, quoting Isaac Felipe Azofeifa provides another very comprehensive definition of research which you should strive to know. She defines research as follows: "Research is a (1) systematic

3. Hancock & Algozzine, *Doing Case Study*, 3.
4. Cresswell, *Educational Research*, 3.

search for (2) adequate information to reach (3) objective knowledge of a (4) specific topic."[5] Let us examine further some of the individual aspects of this definition.

Why is research systematic? According to the definition above, it is systematic because it needs efforts from you as researcher in order for it to be accomplished. It is rigorous in its nature. It also needs clear and logical methods or procedures in order to accomplish it. In this case, research is not easy; it is something that needs time and energy in order to accomplish it.[6]

What is adequate information? According to the definition above, it is the information that emanates from questions or problems existing in the community, not from knowledge emanating from what one just thinks in the mind. This assertion means that one does not need to just seat on a table, think about particular interesting questions, formulate those questions, formulate answers to those questions, and present them. That mere "table work," though a good craft, it is not research and the information provided is not adequate in this sense.

What is objective knowledge? According to the definition above, it is the knowledge that you add to the prior existing knowledge, i.e., the knowledge that you add to what you already know. Always research looks for facts; it looks for unknown facts, not just possibilities or mere personal biases. Objective knowledge, therefore, must be that knowledge you contribute to what others have already done, not just repeating what others have just produced in their researches or reproducing your own emotional experiences. You must first know what others have done, and what you will strive to contribute to that existing knowledge without any personal bias.[7] In order to know what the existing knowledge is, or what others have done and the gap needed to be filled, you have to do what we call *Literature Review*.[8]

What is a specific topic? According to the definition of research above, a specific topic is a theme with a clearly focused problem in it that you need to solve in your research. When we speak of a "specific topic" we mean that the topic needs to deal with only one problem; it should avoid having many problems. This means that the huge topic with many sub–problems is not

---

5. Azofeifa in Vyhmeister, *Quality Research Papers*, 3—4.

6. Page, Barton, Unger & Zappavigna, *Researching Language*, 45.

7. Cf. Myrdal, *Objectivity in Social Research* (1983).

8. The concept of "literature Review" and how to do it are further elaborated under chapters four and six below.

specific. As we have just stated, a specific topic must have only one huge problem to solve.

Fourth, other scholars of research define research as a systematic intervention to search for knowledge in order to build a new theory or test an existing one.[9] Let us also examine closer some of the aspects of this way of understanding research.

What is a theory?

Following the above definition of research, a theory is an explanation about an existing phenomenon, idea, or situation. It is a well–substantiated explanation about a phenomenon, idea or situation that researchers believe to be true. This means that a theory comprises tested hypotheses which are accepted as the bases of the explanation of that particular phenomenon, idea, or situation. It contains an idea "that condenses and organizes knowledge about the social world."[10] In turn the hypotheses are built up of interrelated concepts. Therefore, concepts are building blocks of a particular theory.

What is Theory building?

According to the above definition of research, theory building is the construction of explanations about an existing phenomenon, idea, or situation using the collected data. This is also called "theory after" meaning that data are collected first and a theory systematically developed after that by the use of the collected data. Most qualitative researches are designed for building up of theories from data. Why is a theory built? This is an important question. A theory is build if there is no satisfying or convincing explanation about a particular topic. This means that if there is a satisfactory or convincing theory about a phenomenon, situation or issues existing, there is no need for developing a new theory.[11]

---

9. See Macdonald, *Test Theory* (1999); Glaser & Strauss, *The Discovery of Grounded Theory* (1999).

10. Neuman, *Social Research Methods*, 40; cf. Mligo, *Doing Effective Fieldwork*, 24–25.

11. Punch & Qancea, *Introduction to Research*, 25–26, 168–169.

What is Theory Testing?

According to the above definition of research, theory testing is the measurement of the validity of a particular theory using the collected data. This phenomenon is also called "theory first." The collected data are used here to test the variables that constitute the hypotheses of the existing theory as to whether they are still valid or other explanations should be provided. And variables are operationalized concepts; or stated more precisely, the variable is the operationalized property of a particular object. This means that a theory can be tested in order to see whether it survives the current advancements. In doing that the theory can either be maintained, modified, or rejected outright.[12]

The more significant aspects in a theory are the variables that constitute the hypotheses to be tested. The *"language of variables"* which is contained in hypotheses to be tested is not a research language; in its essence, it is borrowed from mathematics and statistics. This language explains why most researches that are concerned with testing theories (quantitative researches) are mathematical and statistical in nature. Therefore, following the above definition of research, data are always collected in order to build a theory or test the validity of a particular existing theory.

BASIC TYPES OF RESEARCHES

This section introduces the basic types of research. There are different ways of categorizing types of researches; and every research theorist categorizes them according to own preferences.[13] Following Upgade and Shede, in this book we categorize types of research as follows:[14] *first, Research can be Descriptive and/or Analytical* —The question here is the following: What is the aim of research? This question means that research can aim at being descriptive or analytical. On the one hand, the major purpose of descriptive research is providing descriptions of a state of affair, of a phenomenon, and of an idea as it exists. The major characteristic of this type of research (descriptive) is that you just report what has happened in a descriptive form. For example, you can describe the frequency of shopping people do, the major preferences people have, and the causes of existing events. On the

---

12. Ibid., 25–26.

13. See Saldanha & O'Brien, *Research Methodologies*, 14–16.

14. Upgade & Shede, *Research Methodology* (2012).

other hand, analytical research analyzes the existing data and provides a critical evaluation of them.

Second, Research can also be Applied or Fundamental. On the one hand, applied research is sometimes called Action Research and/or Evaluation Research; and Fundamental research is sometimes called Basic or Pure research. Applied research aims at finding a solution for an immediate problem facing a particular community or a particular organization, whereby, on the other hand, fundamental research is mainly concerned with generalizations and formulations of theories using the collected data.

Examples: Researches that concern with natural phenomena or those that relate to pure mathematics are called Fundamental or Pure researches. Researches that are concerned with human behavior and aim at making generalizations about the way human beings behave are also called Fundamental Researches. These researches are of interests to scholars for them to only increase more theoretical understanding about particular phenomena or issues. They have no practical significance. However, researches that aim at certain conclusions or solutions facing a community, industry, or organization are called applied researches because the understanding of the phenomenon studied leads towards solving a particular problem. These researches have a practical significance to the community.[15]

Third, Research can either be Qualitative or Quantitative—The major question here is: What form of data do I need? On the one hand, quantitative research is after data in the form of numbers analyzed by means of numerical comparisons. This approach is applicable to phenomena that can be expressed in terms of quantities (Kiswahili: *kiasi*). Quantitative research evolves from the positivist tradition (paradigm),[16] an approach to knowledge that emphasizes on reality being outside the person (ontology), neutrality (objective endeavor to understand social reality) (epistemology), that is, the distance or separateness of the researcher from what is being researched, and

15. Cf. Johnson & Christensen, *Educational Research*, 6—8. Booth, Colomb & Williams, *The Craft of Research*, 64–67.

16. The word "paradigm" comes from the Greek word "*paradeigma*" which means "*pattern*." In his book The Structure of Scientific Revolutions, Thomas Kuhn was the first author to use the concept of "paradigm" to denote a particular framework which scientists share in finding solutions to problems within a particular time span. A paradigm consists of shared patterns, values and ideas which make it binding to scientists of that particular time. In other words, a paradigm or research tradition includes a research culture which scientists consider appropriate within a particular time(see Mligo, *Doing Effective Fieldwork*, 90).

the universality of science and the method of doing science (method), that is, reality can be studied using the same methodological or investigative logic. In this case, the major aim of quantitative research as a positivist approach to knowledge is to measure the whole by measuring the relationship of its parts using questionnaires and the methods of natural sciences.

On the other hand, qualitative research is after quality (Kiswahili: *ubora*); and data are in the form of words spoken by people researched about their lived experiences, or of words of your descriptions of what you have observed and experienced analyzed by descriptive comparisons of phenomena. It evolves from the interpretivist (interactionism, phenomenology, and ethnomethodology) approach (paradigm) to knowledge that emphasizes on meaning of situations or phenomena as perceived by those who experience them, meanings that are not fixed, but negotiated from time to time. This approach is interested in the way participants explain their experiences in regard to a particular phenomenon which you are interested to study. Qualitative approach, as an interpretivist approach, does not emphasize on distancing the researcher from what is examined; rather, it is more subjective emphasizing on the use of interviews and observations that make the researcher involved in the life and situations of those being researched. In this case, qualitative research is naturalistic whereby reality is constructed by research participants and varies from one participant to another or from one culture to another within groups holding similar understanding.

Cresswell outlines the characteristics of qualitative and quantitative researches basing on what takes place in the research process. According to him, quantitative research has the following characteristics:[17]

1. *Identification of research Problem*—The identification of research problem bases on the trends in the field, or the requirement for the researcher to provide explanations for the reasons of the occurrence of things in a particular place. This means that the relationship between variables characterizes this type of research. Here, the research deals with the way one variable affects another.

2. *Literature Review*—Literature review is significantly done prior to research. Its aim is to justify the need for studying the research problem proposed and the research questions that may be raised for the proposed study problem.

17. Cresswell, *Educational Research*, 11–19.

3. *Research Questions*—Research questions asked are narrow and specific. Their aim is to obtain measurable data focusing on the identified variables within a hypothesis.

4. *Data Collection*—Data collection is done using an appropriate instrument for measuring variables in the hypothesis. The instrument often contains standardized questions, e.g., questionnaires and checklists.

5. *Analysis of obtained Data*—Analysis is done by mathematical procedures known as *statistics*. The analyzed data are presented in terms of numerals in tables, figures, graphs, charts, and histograms.

6. *Reporting of Findings*—In reporting the findings, you will have to follow a predictable format: introduction, literature review, methods or methodology, results, and discussion of the results. This format forms a traditional standardized structure for all quantitative researches.

7. *Evaluation of Research Done*—In evaluating quantitative research one checks whether there is an extensive literature review to justify the problem studied, a good research question and hypothesis for your research, rigorous and impartial methods for data collection, an application of appropriate statistical procedures, a good relationship between the interpretation made and the data obtained (i.e., the interpretation should follow from the data). Therefore, according to Patton, the validity of quantitative research does not depend on the skills of the researcher; rather, it depends on the way the measuring instrument is constructed to measure what it is supposed to measure and its proper administration following the required procedures. The validity of research in quantitative research focuses on the instrument and its administration.[18]

Qualitative research has different characteristics from those of quantitative research. It has the following characteristics:

1. *Identification of research Problem*—The identification of the problem does not follow a particular trend in the field and the variables to be tested are not known. You, as researcher, will need to explore the variables in the course of the study.

2. *Literature Review*—Literature review is not significant at the beginning of the research. This means that it does not provide any directions for the research questions and show the importance of the problem. The

18. Patton, *Qualitative Research*, 14.

research question and the importance of the problem of research will depend on the views of participants and the way you understand them in the course of research.

3. *Purpose and Research questions*—You state the purpose and research questions which are broad and open-ended. It is not necessary to state a hypothesis in qualitative research.

4. *Data Collection*—the data collection process involves you to learn from participants. People you learn from are not "subjects" from whom you draw the data you need for your aim; they are "participants" who share with you their lived experiences. This means that qualitative research involves extensive interaction between you as researcher and research participants.

5. *Data Analysis*—In analyzing data, you break the whole into its parts and figure out how they work together. The data gathered are in the form of text, and the analysis involves the division of the text into segments (groups of related sentences). No statistics are used in qualitative analysis. Analysis is done in the form of words to obtain themes or central ideas contained in the segments. However, data analysis in qualitative researches is an ongoing process; it continues as the data collection process continues. As Patton asserts: "The analysis of qualitative data involves creativity, intellectual discipline, analytical rigor, and a great deal of hard work. Computer programs can facilitate the work of analysis, but they can't provide the creativity and intelligence that make each qualitative analysis unique."[19] This means that while computer software assist the process, especially the final stages, the human being creatively and intelligently does the analysis itself from the beginning of data collection to its end.

6. *Reporting of Findings*—The reporting of findings does not have a predictable format for all qualitative researches. Each qualitative research may have its own logic or format of presentation.

7. *Evaluation of Research*—A good qualitative research requires being realistic and persuasive to convince readers of its credibility. According to Patton, the validity of qualitative research does not mostly depend on the instrument used; rather, it depends on you, the searcher, who conducts the research: your skills, your competence, and your

19. Patton, *Qualitative Research*, 442.

rigor.[20] This is because in qualitative research the researcher is always the *primary instrument* for understanding people's worldviews, perceptions and experiences. The researcher is the one who provides the frameworks of the responses of informants through the skills and competences of questioning and observing.

Therefore, the above characteristics of the two kinds of researches portray the two different paradigms represented by each of them as discussed in the above paragraphs.

Fourth, Research can either be Field and/or Library Research—The major question here is the following: Where is the source of the data I need? The source of data may be from your empirical work done in a particular field. Research done in that way is called *empirical* or *field research*. The source of data can be written materials in a library. This kind of research is called *library research.*

Fifth, research can either be deductive or inductive—The major question here is the following: what do I want to do with the obtained data, or what type of reasoning do I want to follow? Data obtained may be used to infer specific hypotheses to be tested from the general theory, or to make generalizations from a small sample of informants to a larger population. It means that in deductive reasoning the researcher moves from the general to the specific. Deductive reasoning is also called a top—down kind of reasoning. Consider the following example of propositions:

Example: All medical doctors study medicine,

Mwanahamisi studied medicine,

Therefore, Mwanahamisi is a medical doctor.

In deductive reasoning you draw a *specific* conclusion from *general* premises as shown in the example above. In this kind of reasoning, the truth of the conclusion will always depend on the truth of the premises, and so is its falsehood. Therefore, in using deductive reasoning as the bases of your research, you have to be careful with the premises which you base to draw your conclusion.[21]

In inductive reasoning the researcher moves from the specific to the general. Inductive reasoning is also called *bottom—up reasoning*. Here your reasoning moves from the individual to the universal. This kind of

---

20. Patton, *Qualitative Research*, 14.

21. Johnson & Christensen, *Educational Research*, 9.

reasoning is a *probabilistic* kind of reasoning because you examine a small (specific) sample and generalize the observation obtained to the larger population making inferences. In doing that, you are required to assume that the larger (general) population has the same traits as the ones observed in the smaller (specific) sample. In this case, inductive reasoning helps us generalize issues we observe in small samples to the larger populations. However, our generalizations are just probabilities. They are not always necessarily fully convincing.[22]

It follows from the above definitions of research that most quantitative researches which aim at testing general theories using specific hypotheses follow deductive reasoning, while qualitative researches that build general theories from the collection of data from a specific case, phenomenon, or issue follow inductive reasoning.

ASSUMPTIONS, CHARACTERISTICS AND IMPORTANCE OF RESEARCH

Having defined research and outlined the basic types of researches in the previous sub–sections, this section elaborates the basic assumptions you might have when you approach the issue of research, the characteristics of research, and discusses the importance of research for human development.

Basic Assumptions

Assumptions are things that you preliminarily consider being true without checking whether they are true or not. They are just your own beliefs for something to be true even though the evidence that support for their truth is either absent or very limited. In most cases, when we approach the phenomenon of research, we do it with the following assumptions:

i. We assume that events are patterned, so they never occur accidentally or randomly. There is a degree of order and structure in the way reality portrays itself to us. This means that events can be studied and understood.[23]

ii. We assume that the existing nature can be studied and understood. This means that "We can study many parts of reality one at a time,

22. Ibid., 9–10.

23. Koul, *Methodology of Educational Research*, 7.

then add the fragments together to get the picture of the whole."[24] Or, we can interpret the existing nature with our own interpretative ability. Nature includes, but not limited to, human beings and what they always do in their various contexts.

iii. We assume that knowledge is superior to ignorance. However, scientific knowledge is tentative and changing. This means that the things you know today may be known differently tomorrow. Things are not the same everyday. This means that reality is relative and perceived differently by every person, groups of people, or cultures of people. Hence, research is not static, it is dynamic. The same question may have different answers in different places. This also means that since human beings are limited beings (they cannot know everything) scientists engage themselves in a never ending quest for knowledge about the existing reality.[25]

iv. We assume that all natural phenomena have their natural causes. This means that all what we see and experience were caused by nature to be the way they are. Therefore, it is the task of research to uncover or determine why things are, the way they are.

v. We assume that knowledge is acquired through theory and practice. We know differently. Knowledge is embodied *within* us and *among* us. Through hearing from each other and participating in the various practical issues around us, we come to know the world around us. This means that meaning of reality is our own construction. This assumption makes field research an important scientific intervention.

Therefore, basing on the above assumptions, you draw the legitimacy to do research and draw conclusions from the world around you for the sake of advancing knowledge.

Characteristics

Research is a process that involves collecting, analyzing and interpreting data for the advancement of knowledge about existing human problems. As a process of collecting, analyzing, and interpreting research data in order to answer human questions, social research has the following characteristics:[26]

24. Neuman, *Social Research*, 67.

25. Neuman, *Social Research*, 66—67.

26. Upgade & Shede, *Research Methodology*, 3.

a) *It is controlled*—This characteristic means that research is governed by specific scientific procedures that must be followed in order for it to be carried out scientifically. Research is not a random intervention led by human anarchy. It follows prescribed scientific procedures towards its accomplishment.

b) *It is rigorous*—This characteristic means that you must be scrupulous (meticulous, careful, or painstaking) to make sure that the procedures are relevant and earnestly followed in the research process.

c) *It is systematic*—This characteristic means that the procedures followed to do an investigation follow a particular sequence until research is completed. This indicates that there is order in carrying out research.

d) *It is valid and verifiable*—This characteristic means that conclusions reached in regard to the question being researched are logically convincing, and can be verified by other researchers.

e) *It is empirical*—"Empiricism is a philosophical term to describe the epistemological theory that regards experience as the basis or source of knowledge (. . .). Experience refers here to what is received through the senses, to sense data or what can be observed, as well as to the interaction between the person and the world. Thus 'empirical' means based on direct experience or observation of, or interaction with, the world."[27] Philosopher John Locke (1632—1704) is the proponent of this philosophical idea that links knowledge to experience. He conceived that at birth the mind of a person is *tabula rasa;* meaning that it has nothing. This mind is written on as the person grows and perceives the world around. According to this idea, learning comes through one's senses: looking, feeling, hearing, smelling, and tasting. Through the sense perception one comes to understand the surroundings.[28] Therefore, when we say that social research is 'empirical' we mean that it deals with the problem by trying to answer its research question through "obtaining direct, observable information from the world" rather than only using reasons of one's own intellect. It also means that any conclusions which you reach at the end of your research should be based on concrete evidence from information collected from real

27. Punch & Qancea, *Introduction to Research*, 2—3.

28. Johnson & Christensen, *Educational Research*, 8; Punch & Quncea, *Introduction to Research*, 3.

life of people. In other words, as we also noted in the definitions of research above, social research provides adequate information to reach to plausible conclusions about the hypothesis that is being tested or the thesis being argued for.

f) *It is critical*—This characteristic means that it does not allow you to just accept the data obtained and leave them without question. The data collected are subject to scrutiny to verify their validity and reliability in regard to what is investigated. Always researches are critical to particular existing problems. Here it means that the data collected are at the mercy of your analysis and interpretation to provide meaning about a particular phenomenon, idea or situation being researched.

Following the above characteristics of social research, it becomes possible for researchers to evaluate or distinguish between research and mere stories about phenomena.

Importance of Research for Community Development

Having discussed the characteristics of social research in the previous section, the question we need to answer here is the following: Why is research important for human development? Why should researchers spend time and energy conducting research about existing phenomena, idea, or situations around them? In fact, research is important for several reasons. Some of these reasons are the following: First, it provides people voice from what they speak. The saying so goes, "No research no right to speak." This saying means that without research you have no right to speak because you have no data (evidence) to support what you speak. Everything you claim, you must have concrete evidence. Research provides data which is the evidence to support what you speak. In scientific point of view, you cannot speak about the number of people who are poor in Njombe Region in Tanzania if you do not have data. You cannot speak about the problems caused by globalization in rural areas in Sub-Saharan Africa or large industrial cities in Western countries if you do not have data. You cannot speak about the existence of corruption in government offices if you do not have data, and you cannot speak about problems facing people living with HIV/AIDS in your city of residence without having data. This assertion means that research is important in order to provide data for whatever you claim.

Second, research is important for improving the well being of rural and urban societies, countries, and continents. The growth of cities, villages, countries and continents depend on research. The development of hospitals, industries, etc., depends on research. This means that without research there is no development in various sectors of human life. Research involves identification of problems facing communities and finding ways of solving them for the communities' well being.

Third, research is important for countries to formulate policies in regard to the lives of their people. For example, for a country to formulate a plausible budget, it needs to know the population of people it has; and in order to know the population, it needs to do research. That is why census is done regularly in countries to know the number of people residing in those countries in order to plan for their social lives.

Fourth, research is important in business and market operations. Business people are sensitive to demands and supplies of commodities in order to control the fall and rise of prices of their commodities. In order to know the demands and supplies of commodities, they have to do research. In this case, business people are sensitive to the needs of customers and always do research on the way they can satisfy their needs.

Fifth, research is important in solving social problems and hence maintaining the required social equilibrium. Examples of social problems include, but not limited to, the following: lack of adequate relationship among people and stigmatization, and lack of adequate social services. Research enables researchers to discover the obstacles of social equilibrium, and hence rectifying them.

Sixth, research is important for technological advancement. The growth in technology began in Europe in the Nineteenth Century when Europe discovered industries. Until now one can still see the way technology has advanced in various places of the world: the easy communication, the use of computers, the use of telephones, the easy travels throughout the world, and the use of internet making the world to be at our own fingertips. Hence, in order to discover and advance modern technology research is important.

Seventh, research enables students attain academic awards in universities and colleges. In most universities, a student cannot be awarded a certificate, diploma, degree, Masters or Doctorate without doing research and presenting the findings. This means that the student needs to contribute to the existing knowledge before being recognized as specialist in a particular area of study.

Eighth, for professional researchers, research is a means to earn a living. Research is one of their sources of income through research proposals they write and the findings they communicate after research.

Ninth, research is important because it enables the generation of new theories and the testing of existing theories possible. In doing that research contributes to the advancement of knowledge in the world we live.

Therefore, research stands as the fountain of the generation of knowledge, and an important source of solving existing social, economic, political, technological, religious, and cultural problems facing human beings, thanks to research interventions and the curiosity of human mind. As Booth, Colomb and Williams emphasize: "In fact, without trustworthy tested and published research available to all of us, we would be locked in the opinion of the moment, either prisoners of what we alone experience or dupes to everything we hear."[29]

RESEARCH PROCESS

After knowing the importance of research in various sectors, this section examines the research process. The research process describes the way you begin your research, the way of proceeding with it and the way of ending it. In general, the research process describes the major components of research from beginning to end: what do you want to study (the research problem), how do you want to study it (the approach and the design), whom do you want to study (the samples or cases), how will you find information about the problem studied (the method, instrument, tool, or technique) and the validity of the instruments you will use, how will you analyze and interpret the obtained information (data analysis and interpretation), and with whom will you share your research findings and how (audience and dissemination).[30]

The major components of research process are mainly the following: *First, formulation of the Research Problem*—This is the most important step of all because the better and interesting problem one selects, the better is the research. Research problem emanates from the research idea. It must be consequential enough, either theoretically or practically, to merit

29. Booth, Colomb & Williams, *The Craft of Research*, 10.

30. Page, Barton, Under & Zappavigna, *Researching Language*, 47; Efron & Ravid, *Action Research*, 8; Hancock & Algozzine, *Doing Case Study*, 4; Vyhmeister, *Quality Research Papers*, 3–4.

investigation. Though the answer of the problem is not known, you have to know the means (methods) for its investigation. If the means are not known, then the problem is not worth investigating. This assertion means that you have to strive finding a good research idea, developing that idea into a research problem and developing a worthwhile means for attempting to solve it.

Second, reviewing available literature regarding your problem of study—The major purpose of reviewing other people's literature is to gain more knowledge of what others have already done regarding the problem one wants to investigate. In doing a thorough literature review, you will be informed about what is already known about the problem. Being informed about what is already known, you will know what is missing in the researches already done (research gap) which you want to contribute in your own research work

Third, designing your research study—You have to select which design among the existing designs will be used in your research study. You may decide to use another plausible design apart from the existing ones provided that it suggests a promising scientific study of the suggested problem. The research design will describe the whole framework of your research work. It should include the approach for the study (qualitative, quantitative or mixed) and the reasons for choosing such an approach, the method to be used and the reasons for using such method, the type of data expected to be collected in that study, samples and sampling procedures used and why use such procedures. You should bear in mind that the research design in qualitative researches is flexible; it can change in the process of the research but not flexible in quantitative researches.

Fourth, collecting research Information—After planning the research, you will have to execute the planned research design. You will have to collect information in order to address your research problem. In collecting research information (data) you will have to use special valid instruments known scientifically. These instruments include, but not limited to, the following: interviews, observations, content analysis, and Questionnaires. By using these instruments, you will collect both primary and secondary data from sources. Primary data come from primary sources and secondary data come from secondary sources.

Fifth, Organizing, Analyzing, and Interpreting the Obtained Data—The data collected from the field are always random. They include random scripts from interviews, from observations, and from responses of questionnaires. They may also be in the forms of notes from documents. These data need to be organized in logical way and analyzed in order to obtain evidence for your argument.

After the data collection process is over, you need to do what we may call *post data collection scrutiny*. At this stage data are still in the form and language which they were collected. Here you review the setting of your research and the value of the data you obtained. Some questions will be important to ask yourself in the process of data scrutiny: How did the data collection instrument work? Are there any data missing? Why are they missing? What problem that hindered me from obtaining all the required data? Most of all, did I find out what I planned to find out in this research? The answers to these and other similar questions will form the bark of your "limitations" part in the "method chapter" of your research report.[31]

After the post data collection scrutiny, it follows the analysis of the obtained data. What is data analysis? In qualitative researches, done by most social researchers, data analysis is the breaking of data into logical sub–themes that explain the data more clearly and involves the arrangement (coding) of data into categories for easy interpretation. Therefore, after data are collected, they have to be transcribed, well organized, and put into intelligible categories. The categories obtained will have to be interpreted as to what they mean to you in terms of your research problem. The whole of the process stated above is called *raw data processing*.

Before the random data collected are subjected to the post data collection scrutiny, they are transcribed. What is data transcription? In qualitative researches, Data are mostly collected in the form of words and in a language different from that of research. They are even recorded in different ways: note taking, or tape recording with unsystematic form. Data need to be systematically arranged and changed from the form which they were collected to the form suitable for analysis. The process of changing data from the *language* and *form* they were collected to the language of research and form suitable for analysis is called *Data Transcription*. For example, when you change the research information (data) collected using the Swahili language commonly used by people in East Africa into English, the language to be used in my report writing, the data collected using tape recorders into a written text, the whole process is called *transcription*.

Sixth, disseminating the results of your research—The research will be meaningless to people if not communicated. You will require to

31. Patton, *Qualitative Research*, 384.

communicate your findings in an intelligible form for other people to understand what those findings of the research conducted are. This assertion means that you will have to write down an intelligible research report in order to disseminate the knowledge and insights gained through your research work. Since communication of research findings is so important, we devote a chapter in this book for writing a research report.

In the dissemination process, however, you will have to do the following: present the analyzed data and discuss the evidence, and conclude and recommend for further actions. This means that after organizing and analyzing the data, they are presented for discussion. In quantitative researches, data presentation is done by the use of Graphs, histograms, and tables.[32] The major objective in quantitative analysis is to show the relationship between variables; and this is vividly seen in the numerical data presented using the above–mentioned ways.

In qualitative researches, data are presented differently from quantitative researches. They are presented in the form of themes, topics, or cases as extracts from interviews and interpreted in a descriptive detail after presentation. The major objective here is to understand people and their worldviews: their mental categories, their interpretations of social objects around them, their perceptions and feelings, and the motives that underlie their actions in their daily lives.[33]

However, Piergiorgio Corbetta describes quite succinctly how data are presented in qualitative research : "*Results* are presented in accordance with a narrative perspective; episodes are recounted and cases are described, often in the exact words used by the respondents so as to communicate to the reader the vividness of the situations studied without altering the material recorded. The standard procedure is as follows: an argument is put forward and an interview extract is reported in order to support and illustrate the point."[34] This means that the way of presenting data will depend very much on your approach used for research.

The discussion of data entails building arguments, comparing, critiquing, and evaluating the data as they appear in the presentation. Discussion comes after the interpretation of the findings of your research. In interpreting the data, you consider what they mean and the significance they have

---

32. See Kumar, *Research Methodology*, 248–262; Nicol & Pexman, *Presenting Your Findings* (1999).

33. Ary, Jacobs, Sorensen & Walker, *Introduction to Research*, 523.

34. Corbetta, *Social Research*, 281.

to the intended audience. Interpretation entails trying to understand (make sense of) the words spoken by the research participants and the actions (or tacit communication) they did during the data collection process. In discussing the data you write up the report about your research, hence moving to the final stages of the research process.

After presenting and discussing the collected data, you will conclude the research process and provide your recommendations. In concluding the research, you will have to summarize the main findings of the research process, state the discoveries obtained from research and the way such discoveries enable you to test or construct a theory about an existing phenomenon. In concluding the research, you will also have to recommend to policy makers what should be done in order to improve the existing empirical condition and provide a projection for further research on some aspects of your research problem..

CONCLUSION

Our sole concern in this chapter was to discuss the meaning and importance of research as a human intervention. It has been obvious in this chapter that the concept of research has various meanings; however, each one of them focuses on scientific discoveries in order to satisfy human needs. The questioning mind of every human being is the source of curiosity towards finding solutions of surrounding problems. In this case, we have demonstrated in this chapter that research, in its various types, characteristics and processes, is important to human life in various ways—from increasing knowledge about the world to solving the everyday problems of humanity.

FURTHER READING LIST

Ary, Jacobs, Sorensen & Walker, *Introduction to Research*, 35–36
Kothari, *Research Methodology: Methods and Techniques*, 1, 5–7.
Vyhmeister, Quality *Research Papers*, 1–3.
Kumar, *Research Methodology*, 6–7.
Upgade, V. & Shede, A., *Research Methodology*, 1–3.
Hancock, Dawson R. & Bob Algozzine, *Doing Case Study Research* (2011).
Nicol, Adelheid A.M. and Penny M. Pexman, *Presenting Your Findings* (1999).
Myrdal, Gunnar. *Objectivity in Social Research* (1983).
Mligo, Elia Shabani, *Jifunze Utafiti*, 10–12.

Chapter 2

TOPIC, PROBLEM, AND THESIS

".. . a good topic is one the researcher loves. Here, love is a passionate at-tachment to the research and an enjoyment of the research process."
—**Conrad & Serlin**, *The Sage Handbook*, **35**

"*The whole purpose of the research, whatever the approach taken (. . .) is to learn more about the problem being investigated.*"
—**Suter**, *Introduction to Educational Research*, **71**

INTRODUCTION

A LWAYS THE RESEARCH PROCESS discussed in the previous chap-ter starts from somewhere. It starts from wonders and amazements as you see what goes on in a particular situation, what is taken for granted as being the "normal" (what is believed to be true; that is, what is doxological), what people do not understand its cause, and what is interesting to have but potentially harmful. You ask relevant questions about that particular situation, issue or idea in order to investigate further about it. In doing that you move from what is *believed* to be true (doxology), that is, the taken for granted situation, issue, idea, or situation, to what is *known* to be true (epistemology).

In this chapter, we discuss the source of your topic for research, how to formulate a good topic, a research problem from the obtained topic, and a research thesis from a research problem in your process to deal with what is doxological towards what is epistemological. The chapter will also deal with research questions that can be raised in order to investigate the problem and the importance of research intervention for human development. Therefore, this chapter forms the foundation of the research process which the researcher will have to conduct. It ends with some important readings to enable the reader explore further the issues discussed.

CONSTRUCTING A RESEARCH IDEA

Doing research is similar to building a house. "Building a house," Mouton writes, "then, consists of the systematic, methodical and accurate execution of the design. In the process of constructing the house, various methods and tools are used to perform different tasks (laying the foundation, bricklaying, plastering, and so on). Finally, at the end of the process, the building inspector certifies that the house has been built in accordance with the submitted design."[1] The research process starts and ends in a similar way as building a house.

In the research process, you have to start from the research idea and proceed to other relevant stages. What is a research idea? A research idea is a thought or collection of thoughts in one's mind about an existing contradiction or contradictions in people's lives. These thoughts can be generated in people's minds intentionally or unintentionally as they make sense of the existing contradictions in the world around them. They include a wide and general impression of what those people see as stimulating and interesting in their research interests. This statement means that the source of a research idea is people's puzzles or surprises on what goes on around them within their research interests that eventually raise curiosity in their minds. It may be an opinion or belief about something not proved scientifically; and it may be an action or event that is unusual to your eyes as researcher.[2]

1. Mouton, *How to Succeed*, 55.

2. Machi & McEvoy, *The Literature Review*, 14–20, cf. Mann, *Methods of Social Investigation*, 51–53.

This puzzle, wonder, or surprise may emerge from people's own experiences of the current existing situation, their reading of the existing theories, their courses, their interaction with fellow students or researchers, their interaction with supervisors, their scanning of internet materials, their attendance at particular social or academic meetings, etc.[3] As they make sense of what they study from the above interactions, they will raise many ideas that are interesting and fascinating. Therefore, research ideas are thoughts which people have, or that emerge in their minds about a particular phenomenon, issue, or situation that raises curiosity in them towards gaining more knowledge about it. These ideas are normally based on existing contradictions, wide, general, and not well–streamlined.[4]

CONCISE, DESCRIPTIVE, AND FOCUSED RESEARCH TOPIC

After you have determined the research idea, you will have to shape it into a preliminary topic of your research. The topic you shape is a *preliminary topic* because it is not the final topic for your research report. The final research topic will be formulated after the research report has been fully written. A preliminary research topic is a broader statement that contains the research problem within it. A preliminary research topic is a concise, descriptive, and focused subject for your research formulated from your wide and general idea. The main thing that the preliminary topic tells you is where in your field of study or in the secondary literature your research will mainly be based. The preliminary research topic is not the thing that you will investigate in your research process; but it contains that thing inside it. This means that the preliminary research topic is neither an idea (where it emanates) nor the research problem to be solved, nor is it the research thesis to be proved or explained. However, the topic contains all of them (the idea, the problem and the thesis) inside it. We will explain the two concepts (research problem and research thesis) below.

Nevertheless, before explaining those two concepts, let us first answer the following question: what do we mean when we say that the topic is a *"concise, descriptive, and focused subject"* of your research? We should again emphasize, a good preliminary research topic is a focused subject for your research. The process of focusing has to do with narrowing down a broad

3. Mouton, *How to Succeed*, 27–38.
4. White, *Developing Research Questions*, 5.

topic into few manageable aspects. Broad research topics have many interesting aspects in them. This means that you have to move from the more general and broad research topic to the more specific aspect that you can easily manage within a particular time.[5] In moving from the more general topic to the more focused one, you make it concise and to the point.

In focusing your research topic you have to start from your own field, then your interest in that field, then what you specifically want to concentrate on, what you mainly want to focus on, and eventually the perspective or vantage point through which you will study the issue you focused on. For example, you have an idea from your field—*Community Development.* This is a very huge and unfocused idea. It has many interesting aspects in it. You select the most interesting aspect from it—*poverty.* Poverty is very huge; however, you can decide to concentrate on *poverty in Tanzania.* Tanzania is also a huge country with many aspects of poverty. You can decide to focus on *how financial poverty affects teachers in Tanzania. Yet, teachers are a large group. You decide to focus more on primary school teachers.* Then you decide to study financial poverty on the perspective of the life of primary school teachers. This means that the life of primary school teachers becomes your angle, point of view, or perspective to study how financial poverty works in the Tanzanian society. In other words, you study financial poverty in an educational point of view. Now you can formulate a more focused research topic thus: "*Financial Poverty and the Life of Primary School Teachers in Tanzania: An analysis of Its Effects on Their teaching Career.*" Remember this research topic is neither a research problem nor a research thesis to be proved; but it is just a focused research topic that has few manageable aspects in it, including the problem and the thesis.

A good and focused research topic has the following components: First, it has *what* you really intend to research in that topic (*the content of the problem*). This statement means that the reader will clearly see the aspect which you intend to focus on in your research intervention. Second it suggests *how* you will go about researching the problem that is within that topic (*methodology*). This statement means that the topic suggests the way of dealing with the problem in that topic: is it an evaluation, analysis, survey, etc.?[6] Third, it tells *to whom* you intend to conduct your research (*which context or population*). The context appears in the topic to alert the reader about the limits of your research or the research parameters.

5. See Mligo, *Jifunze Utafiti,* 28–29.

6. See the list of verbs in appendix C.

The topic alerts about the context or population because it is impossible for any in–depth research to have no context of concentration. Consider the following examples of "colon" topics used in social sciences and the humanities:[7]

Example Title 1: Financial Poverty and the Life of Primary School Teachers in Tanzania: An analysis of Its Effects on their teaching Work

Example Title 2: Divorce and Remarriage among the Bena of Njombe: Assessing the Role of Civil Laws in the Question of Marriage

In the above examples, "Financial Poverty and the Life of Primary School Teachers" and "Divorce and Remarriage" are the contents of the topics respectively. In both cases, the relationships between the variables you intend to examine are mentioned. These variables speak about what you intend to research.

In the first example, you intend to do an analysis, while in the second example you intend to assess the situation. These are the *"how"* of the topics, the methods which you intend to use in dealing with the content of your title. Moreover, in the first example, the context or population of research is Tanzania, while in the second example is the Bena of Njombe. Therefore, in both topics the three major aspects of a focused topic have been clearly indicated.

After you have formulated a "concise, descriptive, and focused preliminary research topic," you will have to formulate two other important aspects: the research problem and the research thesis which you will be attempting to prove in the process of research. These two aspects are interrelated. You cannot formulate a thesis statement without a problem, and researching a problem goes smoother if you have a research thesis.

WHAT IS RESEARCH PROBLEM?

A research problem is anything that has a difficulty of some sort to you, a phenomenon, situation, idea or physical object that brings a problem to you and you would prefer to investigate and find a solution for it. Research

---

7. A "colon topic" is a topic with the main title and a half title separated by a colon. The formulation of main and half–title is a way of moving from general to specific. The main title indicates the general idea which you want to explore while the half title indicates the specific aspect you want to focus on in your research.

problem is a theoretical or practical gap between what is known and what is not known about a particular phenomenon, idea, situation or physical object.[8] Therefore, the research problem is obtained through asking yourself the question "what." What is it that you do not know in this topic and would prefer to investigate in order to know it? This is an important question in order to find an important research problem from a particular formulated research topic. The problem you formulate will be considered important if it does the following: (i) it makes an invisible problem visible; (ii) it makes the visible problem more understood by those who face it; or (iii) it addresses a riddle or unresolved issue trying to resolve it.[9]

Types of Research Problems

There are two ways you can state your research problem: question form or statement form. We illustrate the two forms of research problems below.

Question Form

When stated in a question form, the research problem appears in one or two clear questions which exactly reflect the content of the research title. What follows after the question(s) is the description of the problem in order to clarify it for readers to understand. The description of the problem can be done in several sentences or paragraphs. Consider the following examples of problems stated in question forms:

1. Why is Malaria prevalent in Njombe Town, Tanzania? (*Here you want to investigate the reasons for the prevalence of the disease*)

2. What makes people dwarf in most mountainous areas? (*Here you want to investigate the thing that causes the existence of a situation*)

3. How can we make students perform better in classes? (*Here you want to investigate the way to improve performance*).

4. When will villagers complete their farming? (*Here you want to investigate a specific time for the task*)

8. Mligo, *Doing Effective Fieldwork*, 52.

9. Cf. Rubin, H.J & Rubin, I.S., *Qualitative Interviewing*, 52; Mann, *Methods of Social Investigation*, 55–57.

Therefore stating the problem in a question form is using the Question words: Why, when, where, which, what, and how depending on your intention towards a particular formulated question.

Sentence form

When stated in a sentence form, the research problem appears in only one or two clearly written sentences. What follows after the research problem is the description of the problem in order to clarify it for readers to understand it well. The description can be done in several other sentences or paragraphs. Consider the following examples of statements of the problem:

1. Tanzania is one of the poor countries in the world (*This statement seeks someone to investigate why it is the poorest, or when will it be rich, or how can we make it rich, etc.*)

2. People in Tanzanian villages do not prefer to use condoms against HIV/AIDS.

3. Students in Universities engage in love relationships with fellow students around against their Students' by–laws.

Therefore, as you can note in the above examples, whether in statement or question form, the research question seeks answers for the *why, where, which, how,* or *what* of something unknown. It means that you will still need to respond to why, which, how, where, when, or what questions depending on your preference and intention.

Guidelines for Formulating a good Research Problem

The question here is this: how can you select a good research problem from the topic you have formulated? In selecting or formulating a good research problem there are some guidelines to follow. First, select a research problem which is *relevant* to your career or discipline of your specialization. This guideline means that you cannot be a community development professional and select a topic or research problem from biology, chemistry, or mathematics, and vice versa.[10]

Second, select a problem which *intellectually stimulates* you as a researcher and you have *interest* on it. This guideline means that if the

10. Efron & Ravid, *Action Research*, 14; Mouton, How *to Succeed*, 39.

problem is not stimulating and interesting to you, it is possible for you to be frustrated when you face difficulties in your research process and surrender it on your way.[11]

Third, select the problem which is *researchable*. This guideline means that the topic you select must have possible data sources that can be obtained within the limits of the research duration. If your research time is one month, the topic will be researchable if it will be possible for you to obtain the required data within this time frame. If it will not be possible to find the required data within this time, then the topic is not researchable.[12] Therefore, in order to determine whether the problem selected is researchable you have to ask yourself four important questions: first, do I have the necessary sources of information to address this problem? Second, do I have the necessary qualifications to investigate the selected problem? Third, do I have adequate time to accomplish the research process within the due date? And fourth, what about finances; does the research process demand the use of finances that I can afford?[13]

Fourth, select the problem which is *important* and *worthwhile* to you and to the community. This statement means that if the issue you propose for research is not a problem to people whom the research is done, then that research is not worthy doing.[14]

Select a problem which will lead to another possible problem. The purpose of any research is not to be an end in itself; rather, it is to be a means to other researches. The solutions to the problem you select should have an ability to lead to other potential problems, hence, perpetuating the research process.

Select the problem which is *suitable* in terms of ethical issues around it. This means that the problem you select should not violet ethical issues surrounding the researcher and the informants. If investigating the problem will cause some physical or psychological harm to the researcher or the informants that kind of problem is not worthy investigating. Issues of informed consent, protection from harm, and privacy of informants are important for you to consider before you select your problem for research.

The major purpose of the above guidelines is to make research as smooth as possible. These guidelines show the reasons why you need to do

---

11. Mouton, *How to Succeed*, 40; Dawson, *Introduction to Research*, 1—2.

12. Efron & Ravid, *Action Research*, 14; Mouton, *How to Succeed*, 40.

13. Vyhmeister, *Quality Research Papers*, 32—33.

14. Mouton, *How to Succeed*, 40.

research yourself from the beginning to the end. You have to have your own idea, formulate your own topic, and your own research problem from your own topic. In doing that you will be able to measure its being researchable, its stimulating potentials, and its relevance to your own career.

Characteristics of a good Research Problem

The question here is the following: How can you know that your research problem is good? In fact it is not easy to determine the goodness of the research problem, especially in the perspective of the readers. Yet, it is possible to evaluate a good problem for research and a bad one, especially on your perspective and the work of research ahead of you. Some of the criteria relating to the above guidelines which can help to distinguish the good problem from the bad one are the following: First, the good research problem must be *relevant* to someone's career or profession. This means that it needs to fall upon one's ability to carry it out. If the problem is within another career other than the one you hold, we will not be confident that you can investigate it successfully because you do not have the necessary skills to investigate it. It does not fall into your career.

Second, it must be intellectually stimulating and interesting to you. This has to do with your enthusiasm about the selected problem. It must demonstrate that you are enthusiastically focused towards it. Enthusiasm helps you to withstand whatever hardships that will emerge in research.

Third, it must be researchable within the time-frame of the research. As it is for any project, research project has a time to begin and a time to finish it. If the problem of research is too complicated, especially in terms of obtaining an adequate instrument to execute it, it will likely take more time to finish. In that sense, the problem is not researchable within the time-frame.

Fourth, it must be worthwhile or important to you and to the community being researched. The importance of the problem has to do with its outcomes. How will the community, you yourself as researcher, and other researchers within that particular field benefit from researching that problem? If it does not indicate any benefit, then the problem is not worthwhile.

Fifth, it must be ethically appropriate in the sense that it is possible to fix ethical issues surrounding it. Issues of informed consent, protection from harm and privacy of participants are necessary in making the problem good. If these issues are difficult to fix, then the problem is not worthy studying.[15]

Therefore, the above criteria will make you a little-beat have a grain of light towards making the problem substantial to you, to those being researched, and to other researchers around your field.

Where will you find appropriate Research Problem?

The student can obtain a good and appropriate research problem from various sources or places. We highlighted them when discussing the sources of the research idea. However, here we will elaborate them further. The first place is from class course works which the student studies in a semester or year. The student needs to be inquisitive. You need to raise questions from what is being taught in order to search for answers. Remember there are always more questions than answers in this world. Therefore, you need to use the assigned homeworks, discussions in groups and in classes, and the teaching of lecturers for raising useful questions for research.[16]

The second place is from magazines, books, journal articles, etc. This requires the student to read extensively and search for what others have not researched and theorized about.[17] "Look for claims that puzzle you, that seem inaccurate or simplistic, or for data that others have ignored or not pursued."[18] What others have not done is called a *gap of knowledge*. So you will have to search for the gap of knowledge or a fault in theorizing from what others have done. Then you can decide to bridge the gap or correct the theorizing in your own research.

In order to find a good problem, you have to read resent materials and recently formulated theories. Books, magazines, monographs, journal articles, etc, you read must be published recently. Otherwise, you will find a problem that others have already worked on; hence, you will not contribute anything significant to the ongoing research about the problem you selected.[19]

The third place is from the field (i.e., community around). You can observe what goes on in the field or community around you and ask relevant

15. Ary, Jacobs, Sorensen & Walker, *Introduction to Research*, 55–56.

16. Axelrod & Windell, *Dissertations Solutions*, 33–35.

17. Axelrod & Windell, *Dissertations Solutions*, 37–39.

18. Booth, Colomb & Williams, *The Craft of Research*, 91.

19. Ary, Jacobs, Sorensen & Walker, *Introduction to Research*, 49.

questions about what goes on there. You can start wondering or being puzzled by what goes on. Then you have to formulate a problem for research from what made you wonder. In this case, your experiences in different angles of your life are the bases for acquiring suitable research problems.[20]

The fourth place is in conferences and academic gatherings through listening at presentations and discussions. You need to be attentive and inquisitive to what other researchers present. This assertion means that you should not take for granted what you hear. You have to raise questions that will lead into a research problem for further investigation.[21]

Therefore, all of the above sources of research problem depend mainly on your hard work. In the above sources you need to pass through all required steps: formulating an idea, narrowing it into a topic, and eventually drawing a research problem from the broadly formulated topic. You are the main determinant of the quality of the research problem to be obtained.

WHAT IS RESEARCH THESIS?

After formulating the research problem, you should know the thesis that guides your investigation process. A research thesis is the preliminary claim of your research work, a preliminary unproved statement which you want to attempt proving through your research work. This statement is the one which you put forth as being true about your research problem at the starting point of your research work (quantitative researches) or in your research work proper (qualitative researches). It is the statement which answers the research question you raised about the problem. In fact, this is the statement you will try to prove or disprove, or defend and stand on it as you advance to the solution of your research problem. This means that your research will provide you with the evidence through which you will check, test, argue for or against your thesis; hence, prove or disprove it. The more the evidence from the data gathered supports it, the more plausible is your thesis, and vice versa.

Research scholar Erik Hofstee offers us a lucid definition of this concept. He writes thus:

> A thesis is a guess, an unproven assertion that you will investigate in your [research]. A thesis can be argued with evidence, or

20. Ary, Jacobs, Sorensen & Walker, *Introduction to Research*, 49.
21. Cf. Axelrod & Windell, *Dissertations Solutions*, 37–39.

(sometimes) it can be empirically tested. If it can be empirically tested, it [is] generally referred to as a 'research hypothesis.' In either case, you are forced to take a clear position regarding the problem you have identified, and to either argue for that position, considering the evidence for and against, or to develop a way of testing it.[22]

Hence, following Hofstee above, a thesis is a position you hold regarding the solution of the problem you stated.

RESEARCH THESIS AND RESEARCH HYPOTHESIS

In the definition of research thesis above, Hofstee introduces another aspect—*research hypothesis*, a proposition (statement) that indicates a relationship between two or more concepts and is lower in abstraction as compared to the theory. Its main function is to bring the theory into a form that can be tested through the identification of concepts within it and turning those concepts into empirically testable variables. A hypothesis can either be alternative or null hypothesis. An alternative hypothesis shows an asymmetrical relationship between variables. Consider the following examples:

1. *Students studying in public colleges perform better than those studying in private colleges.*

The relationship of variables within this first hypothesis is asymmetrical. Hence, it is an alternative hypothesis.

2. *Teachers in private schools perform as better job as those in public schools*

The relationship of variables in this second hypothesis is symmetrical. Hence, the hypothesis is null hypothesis.

On the one hand, a research hypothesis is a thesis to be proved (alternative hypothesis) or disproved (null hypothesis) empirically through data collected from the field of study. The hypothesis is a statement with two variables separated by a verb or a comparative form that indicates the relationship between these two variables. For example, "*The value of Tanzanian shilling decreases as farmers reject to sell their crops internationally.*" This is an alternative hypothesis (thesis) that has two variables to be tested:

---

22. Hofstee, *Constructing a Good Dissertation*, 20.

"The value of Tanzanian shilling" is one variable (dependent variable), and "farmers reject to sell their crops internationally" is another variable (independent variable) of the hypothesis. The verb "decreases" indicates the relationship between the two variables. You can test the relationship between the two variables. You can test the effects of the independent variable upon the dependent variable. You can test empirically through evidence from research whether it is true or not that the rejection of farmers to sell their crops internationally causes the decline in the value of Tanzanian shilling. Therefore, the hypothesis has two main characteristics: first, it is less abstract and general than the theory. This means that it is more concrete and specific as compared to the theory. Second, a hypothesis is tentative or provisional; this means that it is derived from a particular theory and waits to be tested for confirmation or modification.

On the other hand, the thesis is wider than the hypothesis in the manner that it might or might not be tested empirically, but must be argued for or against.[23] This means that all hypotheses are potentially theses but not all theses are potentially hypotheses. Some theses may require you to just defend them without doing empirical research, especially when you conduct conceptual researches.

Examples of Topic, Problem, Question, Thesis (Hypothesis), and Purpose

In the examples below we present the topic of research, the problem identified, the question raised from the problem, and the thesis (hypothesis) to be tested or argued for or against in order to make it clear how the four aspects relate to one another.

Example 1

Research Topic: An Evaluation of the Role of Farmers in Tanzania towards the Decline of the financial status of the Country

Research Problem: There is a decline in financial status of the country

Research Question: What causes the decline in financial status in Tanzania?

---

23. Cf. Ary, Jacobs, Sorensen & Walker, *Introduction to Research*, 40–42; Tomal, *Action Research*, 2; Pyrczak & Bruce, *Writing Empirical Research*, 9–10.

Thesis (hypothesis) Statement: The rejection of farmers to sell their crops in international markets causes the decline in the financial status of the country.

Research Purpose: To study the causes for the decline in financial status in Tanzania

Example 2

Research Topic: Marching Guys as Venders: An Analysis of the Works and Lives of Marching Guys at Njombe Town Tanzania

Research Problem: There is a decline in the economy of marching guys at Njombe town

Research Question: What causes a decline in the economic status of matching guys at Njombe town?

Thesis (hypothesis) Statement: The economic status of marching guys at Njombe Town decreases because the large shops at the town have reduced the prices of their goods.

Research Purpose: To determine the causes for the decline in economic status among matching guys at Njombe Town.

Example 3

Research Topic: A case study of the effects of HIV/AIDS among Youth at Mgendela Street of Njombe Town in Tanzania

Research Problem: There is a decline in the daily economic status of the street.

Research Question: Why is there a daily decrease in economic situation at Mgendela Street of Njombe town?

Thesis (hypothesis) Statement—The daily economic situation at Mgendela Stree of Njombe Town decreases because many strong youth die due to HIV/AIDS

Research Purpose: To analyze the reasons for the decline in economic status at Mgendela Street of Njombe Town

In the examples above, the thesis (hypothesis) statement is your prelimi-nary guess standpoint you believe as being the true answer about your re-search problem and question before doing your research proper. This thesis is the position you expect to argue for or against depending on the evidence of your research. Something important to note here is that once you have identified the research problem from your research topic, you have to raise questions to address that problem and guess the possible answer for the question. That is your Thesis (or hypothesis)! Therefore, the purpose of your research will be to answer the research question you posed, and your preliminary answer (thesis/hypothesis) will remain tentative until research proves it true or wrong.

To our advice, it is easy to deal with one thesis (hypothesis) instead of breaking it into more than one within the same research. Why? It is mainly because each hypothesis will require its own argumentation or testing with a specific method reaching conclusions about it. Doing that will be a laborious task, time consuming, and can lead you into a superficial re-search work. Hence, as Hofstee suggests, the whole of your research about a particular thesis (hypothesis) "should then unfold from your explaining of your thesis, to the reviewing of the secondary literature relevant to it, to the developing of a method to investigate it, to the presentation and analysis of findings regarding it, to your conclusions about it."[24] This is what entails the research process. In the following sub–section we describe the issues that make a thesis (or hypothesis) important in research.

Importance of Thesis (hypothesis) Statement

The thesis (hypothesis) statement is important in research because of the following aspects: First, it "allows researchers to precisely define what they will investigate. (. . .) A thesis statement is a device that allows you to focus on the problem and develop a way to address it. It prevents [you] from meandering all over the place, directionlessly."[25]

Second, the thesis (hypothesis) is a contract between you and your readers. "Your part of the contract is to formulate and delineate the thesis statement, and then to investigate it. The reader's part of the contract is to

---

24. Hofstee, *Constructing a Good Dissertation*, 20.
25. Ibid.

evaluate your work *only* according to the criteria laid down in your thesis statement and method."[26]

Third, the thesis (hypothesis) "gives you clear boundaries and a clear reason to do what you do."[27] The reason in whatever you do will be the following: "It is important and necessary for the assessment of my thesis." A good thesis (hypothesis) always will lead you towards focusing on what you want to do. It also directs you to what is relevant to be done in order to assess it in a proper way to reach conclusions about it.

Fourth, the thesis (hypothesis) "will automatically force you not to write a merely descriptive [research report], which is a thing to be avoided at all costs."[28] We encourage a research report to be analytical and argumentative. In order to be analytical, you have to take a stand or position about the problem at hand. This means that you have to have a thesis (or hypothesis).

The question which can be raised is the following: Should you have to formulate the thesis statement whenever you identify the research problem from your research topic? Here, it is not necessary to formulate it if other previous researchers had a similar problem and formulated a thesis. You may decide to test or investigate the same thesis which was used by previous researchers. However, you should either use a different method of investigation in the same context, or apply the same method they used to a different context of study. In whatever the case, you will reach at generating new knowledge about that thesis, which is the central purpose of every academic research work!

What is important to note is that the thesis (hypothesis) is just an initial guess of the outcome, an initial guess of the answer to the question about the research problem. It is neither a research question nor a statement of the problem itself. Nevertheless, it is a statement that emanates from the research problem which you strive to prove it right or wrong. As Hofstee warns us, "It doesn't matter at all whether you prove your thesis statement right, wrong, or anything in between. Initially it is only a best guess; you don't know the answer and that is why it is worth investigating. You are not going to be judged on whether you have a crystal ball to look into. You

26. Ibid.
27. Ibid.
28. Ibid., 21.

are going to be judged on whether you investigated a worthwhile issue in a reliable manner and came to a well–substantiated conclusion about it."[29]

Important Points about the Thesis of Research

What important points should you bear in mind about the thesis? Hofstee mentions five of them: First, "A thesis statement can't simply name a topic or problem you have identified. It must take a stand about something. It must give you something to argue, to test, to probe, to prove."[30] Remember that the whole research enterprise focuses upon testing or arguing for or against the thesis. It focuses on collecting the evidence to argue for or against it.

Second, "The arguable or testable stand taken in the thesis statement must be one that a person knowledgeable in your field could challenge, argues for or against. If there is no room for disagreement about your thesis, it is not worth investigating."[31] This assertion means that your thesis (hypothesis) must be able to excite other researchers towards finding new knowledge because they will be stimulated to question it and find more knowledge about it.

Third, "A thesis statement cannot be expressed as a question. It is a *statement*, an assertion about something, not a question about something."[32] Remember that it is a statement with measurable or arguable variables—the dependent and independent variables formed by concepts.

Fourth, there is nothing to worry whether the thesis (hypothesis) will be proved right or wrong by the collected evidence. A thesis statement is just an initial guess, or standpoint which you hold on in order to focus you towards what is supposed to be studied.

Fifth, "Try to avoid having a thesis statement that predicts something that may or may not happen in the future. The future hasn't happened yet and that makes it extremely difficult to come to firm conclusions about."[33] This means that the thesis should be concerned about an existing situation, not about the situation anticipated to exist in the future.

---

29. Hofstee, *Constructing a Good Dissertation*, 24.
30. Ibid., 23.
31. Ibid., 24.
32. Ibid.
33. Ibid., 25.

RESEARCH AND DATA COLLECTION QUESTIONS

In the previous sub–sections of this chapter we discussed about formulating research topics from research ideas, research problems from research topics, and research thesis (hypothesis) from research problems. After you have managed to do all of the aspects listed above, you will now need to formulate a research question from your research problem.[34] A research question is the one which you will focus on in your research process. Scott and Garner have the following on the importance of research question for empirical studies: "Without a guiding research question (or cluster of related questions), empirical studies would be reports of mere observations, at best entertaining to read but more likely amounting to a disorganized set of field notes or a hot mess of aimless numbers. The research question motivates and structures data and their collection, the process of analyzing data, the creation of theories to make sense of the data, and the composing of a story that brings all together."[35]

The research question you formulate must be *challenging*. This means that it should not be answered by only "yes" or "no" answers. Moreover, it should not be answered by the provision or dictionary definitions, or by just presenting issues highlighted in the textbook. You need to reformulate your research question to make it challenging. A challenging research question raises your curiosity and urge to know more about the asked issue. In other words, it provokes thought and engages you in a debate. In this case, if the question you have formulated does not fulfill this task, you will have to reformulate it to address this task.

The words in the above paragraphs show that a research question is a yardstick to guide the research towards focusing on what is designed to investigate because it organizes the project and provides it direction, provides boundaries to what you do in the research project, enhances you towards focusing on a specific issue of investigation, provides to you a framework for reporting on the project executed and points to the data that will be expected to answer that question.[36] Therefore, the "good research question has the following characteristics: it is feasible, has social importance, is

---

34. Cf. White, *Developing Research Questions*, 33—35.

35. Scott & Garner, *Doing Qualitative Research*, 32 .

36. Ibid.

relevant, is ethical to participants, and is clear."[37] It should be worth asking and capable of being answered using scientific procedures.

Nonetheless, there is a distinction between the *main research question* and *data collection questions* which requires your close attention. Punch and Quncea state this distinction more clearly when they write: "A research question is the question that guides the project, and which the research is designed to answer. A data collection question is more specific again, and is a question that is asked (for example, in a survey questionnaire or interview) to provide data relevant to a research question."[38] Peterson also states thus regarding research and data collection questions,

> Unless the researcher asks the right questions in the right way, a research project will not produce useful information, no matter how well other research aspects are designed and executed. Even worse, improper questions or questions asked improperly will most likely result into invalid and unreliable information—information that virtually guarantees an incorrect decision, a poor theory test, or misinformation about a topic.[39]

Therefore, the statements by Punch and Quncea and Peterson above highlight for the need of having both types of questions in order to accomplish research. You have to ask the right questions rightly in order to accomplish your research work.

However, you have to note that there is also a difference between questions on qualitative researches and research questions in quantitative researches. In qualitative researches questions are broader; they are open ended questions. The respondent does not need to answer yes or no. They require some descriptions. They are mostly "how" and "which" questions. In quantitative researches question seek for the amount, they are mostly "how much" or how many" questions. They are questions that measure the quantities of things.[40]

37. Mligo, *Doing Effective Fieldwork*, 30.

38. Punch & Quncea, *Introduction to Research*, 87.

39. Peterson, *Constructing effective Questionnaires*, 13.

40. Efron & Ravid, *Action Research*, 3–32.

Main Research Questions

In the following examples, we will mostly concentrate on qualitative main Research questions and their respective types.

Examples:

Research Topic: Divorce among Christian Marriages in Njombe Town

Possible Main Research Questions:

1. Why are there frequent divorces among Christians in Njombe Town? (*Here the major focus of research is to determine the reasons for the frequent divorces*)

2. How are divorces done among Christians in Njombe Town? (*Here the major focus of research is to determine the means or ways used to effect divorces*).

3. Where do Christians send their divorce cases? (*Here the major focus of research is to locate places where Christians send their divorce cases*).

4. When are divorces more frequent among Christians in Njombe Town? (*Here the major focus of research is to determine the time at which divorces appear more frequently*).

The questions above state clearly that the formulation of the main research question needs you to be careful, determined, and focused. You must know clearly what you want to research on (the problem), and should focus on that aspect throughout the research process. If the main focus is to determine the *reasons*, then the Main research question should focus on reasons. If it is finding means or ways, places, time, etc., the question should focus on these aspects more clearly. Therefore, we can say that the main research question is the foundation of the whole research. The more carefully and focused the question is formulated, the greater it promises for a good research and its outcomes.

All examples of main research questions provided above are empirical questions. Since research questions are formulated from research problems, and research problems are viewed as *empirical* (practical) or *non–empirical* (theoretical), we now explore further about the types of empirical and non–empirical research questions which you can formulate for your research.

Empirical Research Questions

Johann Mouton categorizes six types of empirical research questions:[41] The first type is *exploratory* questions. Your main aim in this type of questions is to explore or make discoveries about a phenomenon, issue or situation. Here you can explore the key factors that lead to the success of a particular case, e.g., company, school, etc. Therefore, in exploratory questions your main concerns are the key factors or features.

Examples:

1. What are the main factors of a successful bank
2. What are the distinguishing features of an effective head teacher in primary schools?
3. What are the key features of a good tourist centre?

The second type of empirical questions is *descriptive* questions. In this type of questions, your main aim is to provide a description of a phenomenon, issue, situation, or case. Here you answer the question "how," or describe the correlation between two items.

Examples:

1. How many people suffer from T.B disease in Njombe Town this year?
2. Is there any correlation between T.B and HIV/AIDS diseases?
3. How much time do youth spend for dancing at Mbeya city?

The third type of empirical questions is *causal* questions. These questions ask the question "why" and "what." Your main concern in these questions is to determine the reason or thing that causes the existence of a particular situation or issue.

Example:

1. What are the causes for the resurgence of malaria disease in Njombe Town?
2. Why are there so many street children in urban areas?
3. What causes the persistence of poverty in developing countries?

41. Mouton, *How to Succeed*, 54—55.

The fourth type of empirical questions is *evaluative* questions. In these questions you focus at assessing the outcome (success or failure) of a particular intervention or programme.

Examples:

1. What is the outcome of the newly introduced ARVs towards reducing HIV/AIDS-related deaths?

2. Has the introduction of mobile phones improved communication in rural areas?

3. What are the successes and failures of the clean water project at Iringa municipality?

The fifth type of empirical questions is *predictive* questions. In these questions you focus on what will happen in the future. You focus on examining the effects which one aspect will have on another. Therefore, you ask the question "what" while focusing on the future outcome.

Examples:

1. What will be the effects of computer technology to primary school pupils in Tanzania?

2. What will be the consequences of drinking unsterilized water to children in nursery schools?

The sixth type of empirical questions is *historical* questions. Here you ask the question "what" caused a particular outcome in the past.

Examples:

1. What caused the rise of freedom movements in Africa in 1960s?

2. What led to the civil war between the Hutu and Tutsi of Rwanda and Burundi?

As you can note, the questions discussed above are empirical (practical) because they involve a particular community in one way or another. Moreover, the outcome of the research done is not only for knowledge gain, but also for improving a particular existing situation in that community. They address the problem in a more practical level.

Non-empirical Research Questions

Mouton also provides four types of non–empirical questions that need our attention.[42] Non–empirical questions do not aim at improving a particular practical situation in a community; their primary aim is to increase knowledge about an issue or phenomenon. The first type is what he calls *meta–analytical* questions. These questions examine the state of knowledge or current research on a particular phenomenon, issue, or situation.

Examples:

1. What is the current research on HIV/AIDS–related stigmatization in sociological studies?
2. What are the key debates among scholars about religion and culture in Africa?
3. What paradigm does the inculturation debate in Africa belong?

The second type of non–empirical questions is *conceptual* questions. In these questions you focus on exploring the meanings of concepts and the way you can apply them in a particular field.

Examples:

4. What does it mean by "tax evasion" and "tax avoidance" in legal applications?
5. What does it mean by "counseling loss" in counseling psychology?
6. What does it mean by "informed consent" in empirical research?

The third type of non–empirical questions is *theoretical* questions. These questions explore current theories or explanations about phenomena, issues or situations.

Examples:

1. What is the widely accepted theory on social interactions?
2. What is a convincing explanation on classroom management?
3. What model can better explain the existence of God?

---

42. Mouton, *How to Succeed*, 54–55.

The fourth type of non–empirical questions is *philosophical* questions. These focus on the ideal or normative states of issues. They seek for meaning of ideas in an abstract level possible.

Examples:

1. What does it mean by Martin Buber's I–Thou relationship among human beings?
2. Do animals speak out their rights?
3. Where do leaders acquire authority to rule over other people?
4. Is the visible world real?

Specific or Data Collection Questions

After you have formulated the main research question, formulate the Specific (data collection) Questions. These are several questions which all address the main research question. These questions focus on small specific issues that contribute in answering the main research question. In most cases, these are questions which you ask informants in the field. Hence, the empirical and non-empirical main research questions formulated above can each one be broken into several specific or data collection questions depending on your need and the type of main research question you have. Consider some of the examples below.

Example 1:

Main Research Question: "Why are there frequent divorces for Christians at Njombe Town in Tanzania?"

Specific (data collection) Questions:

1. How long do Christian marriages last in average?
2. How do Christian married partners relate in their married lives?
3. What binds people in married life?
4. How does procreation affect married life for Christians?
5. How do wealth affect Christian marriages?

45

Example 2:

Main Research Question: "How are Divorces done for Christian Marriages in Njombe Town?"

Specific (data collection) Questions:

1. What is the best way to divorce a Christian spouse?

2. Why do you think this is the best way?

Example 3:

Main Research Question: "Where do Christians send their Divorce cases?"

Specific (data collection) Questions:

1. Do Christians send their divorce cases to civil courts?

2. Do Christians send their marriages to church marriage councils?

3. Do Christians solve their divorce cases for themselves?

Example 4.

Main Research Question: "When are divorces more frequent among Christians at Njombe Town?"

Specific (data collection) Questions:

1. Do Christians divorce more during Easters?

2. Do Christians divorce soon after marriages?

3. Do Christians divorce after acquiring much wealth?

4. Do Christians divorce when they encounter life hardships?

As you can see in the examples above, specific research questions explore more about the main research question. They search for specific answers about specific aspects of the main question of the research.[43] In this case, you can use specific research questions for interviews and questionnaires in the research process. Specific research questions can also be the base

---

43. For more examples on the research question and the data collection questions see Leedy & Ormrod, *Practical Research*, 157–158.

of chapters during the writing stage because each of them searches for a specific aspect or issue about the main question.

CONCLUSION

This chapter has exposed you to some important foundational elements of research: the research idea, topic, problem, thesis, and questions. The knowledge of these preliminary elements is essential for the student and re-searcher to manage designing research intervention. Both the student and the experienced researcher have to know how to find an idea for research, how to turn the huge idea into a focused research topic, how to change the topic into a researchable research problem, how to turn the problem into questions and theses for study. These elements form the foundation of the research process. Moreover, the student or researcher needs to understand the reasons for doing research and the importance of research for human development. This chapter has covered all these aspects. Therefore, the mastery of the aspects discussed in this chapter will enable you to select a suitable research design for research intervention.

FURTHER READING LIST

Efron & Ravid, *Action Research in Education*, 31–38.
Scott & Garner, *Doing Qualitative Research*, 31–50.
Mligo, *Doing effective Fieldwork*, 50—63.
Panneerselvam, *Research Methodology*, 10–11.
Taylor & Ghoshal, *Research Methodology*, 16–18.
Axelrod & Windell, *Dissertations Solutions* (2012).
Page, Barton, Unger & Zappavigna, *Researching Language and Social Media* (2014).
McDonald, *Test Theory* (1999).
White, *Developing Research Questions* (2009).

Chapter 3

SELECTING SUITABLE RESEARCH DESIGN

"Design sits between the research questions and the data, showing how the research questions will be connected to the data, and what tools and procedures to use in answering them. Therefore design needs to follow from the questions, and fit in with the data."

—**Punch & Quncea,** *Introduction to Research,* **144**

INTRODUCTION

ONCE YOU HAVE DETERMINED THE research problem, questions and thesis for your research, your next step is to select an appropriate research design. Remember research intervention is similar to building a house. A good house needs to be built on a good foundation. In order to have a good foundation, several tools and methods have to be used: bricks and brick laying methods, sand, cement, etc and how to prepare them for the foundation. Constructors use the known ways of making a foundation in their own ways. Therefore, when the foundation is over, it determines the quality of the whole house that will emerge from that foundation.

Research design plays a foundational role for the research intervention. You have to prepare a good foundation for your whole research process. This assertion means that you need to select the appropriate approach and type of research you will use in order to answer your research questions, which will eventually lead to dealing with your research question. The selection of the better approach is an exciting step for you because the better approach and type of research you select the more reliable and efficient will be your research outcome. In this case, this chapter exposes you to the meaning of research design, its importance in research, the three main approaches to research, and the types of designs you may use in your planned research.

WHAT IS RESEARCH DESIGN?

Research Design is the *how* part of the research. The research design answers the question: "What type of study do you undertake in order to deal with your identified research problem?" It describes the approach which you select to use in order to deal with the problem of research, and the type of design in that approach. It describes the conceptual (theoretical) framework which you will use in that approach and design selected. It describes the procedures or steps in that type of design that you will use in order to do the anticipated research. It means that research design sets the logic of research. It sets what begins, then what follows, and what ends the research process. Generally, research design answers four main questions: what approach will you use in your research and why, within what theoretical framework, from whom will data be collected and how, and which ethical issues will you take into account in collecting research data?[1]

Moreover, research design provides various methods for collecting data, the samples and sampling procedures, the presentation and analysis of data obtained, and the ways you will write your research report. The type of research design selected provides the plan of the whole research from the beginning to the end. This means that research design is very important; as we said earlier; it is like a foundation of a house. Hence, a research without a proper design is like a house without a proper foundation.

---

1. Punch & Quncea, *Introduction to Research*, 142 –144.

IMPORTANCE OF RESEARCH DESIGN

As the foundation of a house is, research design is important because of the following aspects:

a) It tells us what the research is all about.

b) It tells us where the data will be found.

c) It tells us where you will do your research.

d) It tells us how much time you will use in doing your research.

e) It tells us how much materials will be used in order to make the research successful.

f) It tells us which techniques, or instruments, or methods of research will be used in the data collection process.

Therefore, as building a house requires a properly constructed foundation, a well–planned research also requires a properly selected and used research design. It also requires a proper description of the various issues involved in that particular design or research framework.

TYPES OF RESEARCH DESIGNS

In most cases, a particular research design is located in a particular research approach. Research approaches are mainly three depending on your preference: *Qualitative*, *Quantitative*, and *Mixed* methods approaches. The research design can fall into one of the three approaches. Selecting the approach to use, however, depends on the purpose which your research will serve. You have to select a qualitative approach if the purpose of your research is:

a) Providing a description of a phenomenon, issue or situation in order to reveal their multifaceted nature,

b) Providing interpretation of a phenomenon, issue or situation in order to acquire new knowledge about them or develop new theoretical perspectives about them,

c) Verifying and testing the validity of particular existing assumptions, explanations (theories) or generalizations within a particular context,

d) Providing evaluation or judgment of the effectiveness of particular existing policies, practices and even advancements.

This means that qualitative researches are not concerned with answering questions about cause and effect relations indicated by variables of hypotheses. Questions such as: what causes the existence of a particular phenomenon, issue or situation, are questions of concern in quantitative researches.[2]

You have to select a quantitative approach if your purpose of research is to examine the relationship of variables within a particular hypothesis. In an experimental research design, for example, the cause and effect measurement is the key element. It means that in quantitative researches you may be interested in examining the various possible factors that caused the existence of a particular phenomenon, issue, or setting in order to provide explanations about them.[3]

You have to select a mixed methods approach if your purpose is to use both qualitative and quantitative approaches in your research. You may carry out your research basing mainly on the quantitative approach, but supplement it with the qualitative approach and vice versa. You may use both methods at equal footing. In whatever the case, a mixed method approach uses both qualitative and quantitative approaches in a single research.

In the following paragraphs we briefly outline some of the research designs you may select for your research and what they purport to accomplish in a particular research intervention.

Case Study research Design

Case study is a qualitative research design. The main concern of this design is to work on a particular case you have selected. This design is used to acquire in–depth knowledge about that particular case. A *case* may be a particular social unit, a person, a family, an institution, or a cultural group. It may be a school, a classroom, a football team, an incidence (e.g., a riot, a traffic accident), etc. The main characteristic of a case study design is the focus on *only one* unit and studying it in detail within its particular context. Case study design is used when you intend to acquire a detailed knowledge about the selected case.[4]

2. Leedy & Ormrod, *Practical Research*, 234.

3. Ibid., 234.

4. Swanborn, *Case Study*, 1–5, Hancock & Algozzine, *Doing Case Study* (2011); Fraenkel, Warren Hyun, *How to Design and Evaluate*, 434–435; Yin, *Case Study* (2003).

Extended Literature Review Research Design

This type of qualitative study is undertaken in order to provide an overview of the existing scholarship in a particular field of study. What it does is to relate the various specialties around a particular issue. Substantially, this research does not produce any new knowledge. It jus assesses the existing one. In that case, most researchers do not use it because what it does is to just provide a new perspective in reviewing the literature not a new knowledge about the issue in question.

Survey–based Research Design

Survey–based design is a study design within quantitative descriptive approaches "which you administer a survey or questionnaire to a small group of people (called *sample*) to identify trends in attitudes, opinions, behaviors, or characteristics of a large group of people (called *population*)."[5] You undertake this type of research if you intend to obtain data from a limited number of people who are considered to have the data you seek. These people must be willing to communicate the data and are presumed to be representatives of the larger area of research which the research needs to provide a description (population validity). In this design, questionnaires, checklists, and interviews can be used as instruments of data collection.[6]

Grounded Theory Research Design

This design is also called "Theory Development Research design." In this kind of research design, data are collected in order to generate theory. This design is called "grounded theory" because the theory produced will be grounded on the data obtained from research. The major emphasis of this design is generating a new theory from data collected from the research work, or using the data collected to test the existing theory in order to refine it or provide new explanations about it. What you do with data in this research is to find conceptual categories in the data, find the relationship between these categories, and account for that relationship in a more

---

5. Cresswell, *Educational Research*, 21.

6. Fraenkel, Warren & Hyun, *How to Design and Evaluate*, 398–413; Fink & Kosecoff, *How to Conduct Surveys* (1985).

abstract theoretical level. Different research techniques can be used in this design, both qualitative and quantitative techniques.[7]

We cherish the great people such as Karl Marx, Weber, Freud, Einsten, Newton, Bohr, Darwin, Plato, etc., for their theories. They collected data in order to develop explanations about the world around us. Their theories are not perfect; however, they are influential ones in our continuous search for truth about the world around us.

Evaluative Research Design

As the name suggests, this type of research design seeks to evaluate the effects, successes or failures of a certain intervention. The intervention may be a project, an event, etc. Both qualitative and quantitative approaches may be used to do the evaluation. The design leads you towards answering the question: Why was there a failure or success on the intervention. In this case, this type of research is an appraisal venture, and can either be qualitative or quantitative in nature!

Secondary Data Analysis Research Design

Secondary data are data collected and analyzed by various researchers for their own research purposes. This research design focuses on analyzing secondary data in order to answer your questions. These secondary data can either be qualitative or quantitative. There is a large number of data: dissertations and theses in libraries, financial data, weather data, data in websites, etc. The quality of secondary data will depend on you who analyze them and your aim.

Experiment Research Design

This research design uses samples to test a particular phenomenon. Experiments are done in laboratories or fields. Field experiments use samples to

---

7. Ary, Jacobs, Sorensen & Walker, *Introduction to Research*, 33; Fraenkel, Warren & Hyun, *How to Design and Evaluate*, 433—434; Glaser & Strauss, *The Discovery of Grounded Theory* (1999); Strauss, *Qualitative Analysis* (1987); Glaser, *Theoretical Sensitivity* (1978).

test a certain hypothesis or theory. Both laboratory or field researches can either be qualitative or quantitative in their approaches.[8]

Content Analysis Research Design

This research design aims at closely examining the content of preserved written documents. The design uses various techniques in order to discover the hidden meaning of a record or document, e.g., minutes, diaries, reports, textbooks, letters, websites, etc.[9] This research design is therefore qualitative in its approach.

Comparative Analysis Research Design

In this design you compare two or more things or situations. Your main concern is to investigate in a focused and systematic way the existence of similarities and differences between them, and the reasons for such similarities and differences. The comparative analysis study compares small cases. The difficulty with this design is on the selection of cases to compare, the complexity of each case, and the difficulty in focusing the research.

Ethnographic Research Design

Ethnographic research design is qualitative research design and is sometimes called *Participant observation research design* or *Life History research design* because you as researcher become involved in the activities of a particular group of people being researched in order to understand how that group experience life. This research design is designed to provide a descriptive portrait of people and their cultures. This involves an extensive work in the field; that is, you have to stay in the field of research for a long time studying the chosen group of people. Therefore, the study incurs great costs and is time consuming.

During the research process, you use both formal and informal data collection methods and techniques. Such techniques include, but not limited to, the following: observation, interviews, and documentary records.

---

8. Field and Hole, *How to Design* (2003); Gerber and Green, *Field Experiments* (2012).

9. Ary, Jacobs, Sorensen & Walker, *Introduction to Research*, 32—33.

The main emphasis of this research design is studying the *social cultural life* of a particular community where the research is conducted. The design aims at exploring the "culture" of the people and the way such people live in that culture.[10]

Interdisciplinary Research Design

This type of research design links two disciplines in terms of methods, concepts, or ideas used. One discipline takes those aspects from another discipline and uses them to solve a certain problem from it. For example, a discipline of theology can take ideas, methods, or concepts, from social psychology and use them to solve a problem in it. However, this way of doing needs creativity and carefulness.

Critical Theory Research Design

As the name suggests, a critical theory research design fosters the practice of "critique" to existing situations that are taken for granted and leads to an emancipating type of research. It achieves this goal of being a tool for emancipation through analyzing critically the taken-for- granted social arrangements leading to transformation.[11] In most cases, this research design is more political oriented.

Narrative or Historical Research Design

This is a qualitative research design. The main intention of this design is to understand a past phenomenon by providing a detailed account of it in narrative form. It examines the event in the past and the way in which it illuminates the understanding of the present situation. The main sources for this type of study are written documents that speak about that event. It may be a single event being studied or an array of events or people that lived in the past. A good example of this design is seeking to understand the biographical account of a person or people and explain it in a narrative form. Narrative or historical studies always aim at shedding light to the

---

10. Scott & Garner, *Doing Qualitative Research*, 111–124; Fraenkel, Warren & Hyun, *How to Design and Evaluate*, 435; Gobo, *Doing Ethnography* (2008).

11. Efron & Ravid, *Action Research*, 42; Harvey, *Critical Social Research*, 3–32.

present situation, or strengthening parts of the arguments about the present issues.[12]

Correlation based Research Design

Correlation based research design is one of the designs in the quantitative approaches to research. In this design you use statistical data to compare two or more variables of the hypothesis. What you do is to determine whether there exists a relationship between them. The relationship can either be positive or negative. This design is one of the designs in the descriptive type of research because it usually describes the existing relationship between two variables by using a correlation coefficient (i.e., statistical representations that show the way through which two variables relate to each other).[13]

Action Research Design

This research design, as qualitative research design, is also known as participatory or applied research design because it involves participants in the research process with the aim of solving an immediate problem facing the community. Participants become interlocutors in the process of research in order to solve a particular problem. This design forms a typical collaborative research. Participants are involved in planning, implementation and evaluation of the research results. In doing that, action research focuses at empowering participants. In this way, participants become co–researchers instead of being objects of research.

Three things are notable in this research design: researches are in most cases situated in local contexts and focus on dealing with local issues, researches are done by the practitioners for their own gains, and the result in this kind of research enhances a particular action towards the problem researched or a change in a situation. Therefore, action research is an action–reflection cycle. You as a participant will have to act and reflect on what you act, and undergo changes in the research process.[14]

---

12. Ary, Jacobs, Sorensen & Walker, *Introduction to Research*, 33–34; Fraenkel, Warren & Hyun, *How to Design and Evaluate*, 432; Andrews, Square & Tamboukou, *Doing Narrative Research* (2008)

13. Fraenkel, Warren & Hyun, *How to Design and Evaluate*, 331–357.

14. Ary, Jacobs, Sorensen & Walker, *Introduction to Research*, 548–586; Efron & Ravid, *Action Research*, 4; Fraenkel & Warren & Hyun, *How to Design and Evaluate*,

Phenomenological Research Design

Phenomenological research design is qualitative in nature. The term "phenomenology" means the study of phenomena. Phenomena may be events, situations, concepts, or experience that people face at a particular time in a particular place. The world we live has many phenomena. For example, poverty, stress, deforestation, alcoholism, unemployment, soil erosion, etc. All these aspects are phenomena that one can draw a research problem and conduct research. You, as researcher who use this design, will have to emphasize on *experience* that people have about that phenomenon. The design aims at searching for the way people can describe their experiences of a phenomenon. Therefore, in phenomenological research design, the method used and the samples of people to be researched need to emphasize on the acquisition of people's *experience* about a particular phenomenon.[15]

CONCLUSION

This chapter has shown that research design is as important as the foundation of a house is. You cannot have good research results if you do not know the techniques or methods for researching the problem, you do not know where will the data be obtained, how much time will be used, and where will the research be conducted, and why. These are important foundational research aspects that form the research design. In this case, through the various traditional research designs outlined, this chapter has demonstrated that formal research is hardly possible without a concrete research design.

FURTHER READING LIST

Mligo, *Doing Effective Fieldwork*, 96–107.
Mouton, *How to succeed*, 143–180
Hofstee, *Constructing a Good Dissertation*, 2006.
Fraenkel & Hyun, *How to Design and Evaluate Research,* 432–435
Tomal, *Action Research for Educators*, Second Edition (2010).
Ary, Jacobs, Sorensen & Walker. *Introduction to Research in Education*, Ninth Edition, 28–34, 546–586.
Yin, *Case Study Research*, Third Edition (2003).
Fink & Kosecoff, *How to Conduct Surveys* (1985).
Swanborn, *Case Study Research* (2010).

589–609; Tomal, *Action Research* (2010).

15. Fraenkel, Warren & Hyun, *How to Design and Evaluate*, 432—433.

Gerber & Green, *Field Experiments* (2012).
Field & Hole, *How to Design and Report Experiments* (2003).
Barbour, *Interpreting Qualitative Research*, 228–254.
Harvey, Lee. *Critical Social Research* (1990).
Andrews, Squire & Tamboukou (eds.). *Doing Narrative Research* (2008).

Chapter 4

DEVELOPING SCIENTIFIC RESEARCH PROPOSAL

"The first principle of grantsmanship [or review at an academic institution] is to recognize that a good proposal is an argument . . . for the researcher's project. The proposal must make a case to the granting agency [or a reviewer at an academic institution] that the research question is interesting [and] that the study is important . . . Thus the proposal must be written persuasively."

—**Morse in Silverman,** *Doing Qualitative Research,* **190**

INTRODUCTION

AFTER YOU HAVE SELECTED A SUBSTENTIAL design for your research, you will have to write a scientific research proposal to propose what you want to do, why you want to do it, how you want to do it, what are the cost implications involved, and who has done a similar thing as the one you propose to do in your research proper. In preparing the research proposal, you expand the *how* part of your research design discussed in the previous chapter towards a more scientific document that outlines the proposed activities of the research from its beginning to its end. This chapter devotes on the discussion of what a research proposal really is as an academic document. The chapter also discusses its components and the importance of revising it after finishing the first draft in order to make it more appealing and easy to read and understand what you propose. In this case, the chapter indicates a move from your conceptualization of the research process towards documenting it in a more academic way.

WHAT IS RESEARCH PROPOSAL?

A research proposal is not a research report, though it needs a survey of a substantial amount of literature and presenting it in the form that is academically acceptable. Moreover, a research proposal is not a research design. Research proposal is more than a mere research design; it is a document you prepare for the purpose of outlining the details about a particular research project, including the aspects of the selected research design. In most cases, the research proposal provides explanations about the following aspects:

a) The proposed research itself. It tells clearly what will be done in the proposed research process.

b) Methods and techniques to be used during the execution of research. It tells how the proposed research will be conducted.

c) The importance of the proposed research to you, to the community as a whole and to other researchers. It tells why that research should be done.

d) How much time will be used for conducting the research proposed?

e) It tells the costs to be incurred in order to accomplish it.

This means that the well–written research proposal will show the reviewers that you know what you seek to accomplish, how to accomplish it, and how much will it cost you in terms of finance and time. It shows that you know quite well the main idea surrounding your research being proposed. This means that "the proposal describes what the proposed research is about, what it is trying to achieve and how it will go about, and what we will learn from that and why it is worth learning."[1]

1. Punch & Qancea, *Introduction to Research*, 357.

In a general sense, the research proposal document does the following four notable aspects:

a) It provides a logical presentation of your main research idea,

b) It illustrates the significance and worthiness of that idea for scientific inquiry,

c) It shows the idea's relationship to past researches, and

d) It articulates the activities for the proposed research project in relation to that idea

Therefore, research proposal is an important academic or scientific document because it summarizes academically/scientifically the whole content of research process that you will follow in order to achieve your research goal.

RESEARCH PROPOSAL AS AN ACADEMIC DOCUMENT

Any research proposal is an academic or scientific document. What do we mean by the concepts "academics" or "scientific"? Hofstee explains these concepts more clearly when he writes that the concept "academics"

> is all about coming to new discoveries about ourselves and the world around us. All good academic [or scientific] work attempts to find possible answers to unanswered questions. That means researchers are in the business of explaining the unexplained. They come up with theories to make sense of the world around us and with solutions to practical problems.[2]

In fact, what drives researchers to engage in academic work is the search for new knowledge about existing situations. Therefore, a research proposal is an academic or scientific document because it proposes a search for new knowledge about an existing phenomenon; it proposes for the search of answers about unanswered or incompletely answered questions about human life; or it proposes to explain the unexplained. And in proposing that, the proposal follows all rules of the academic game outlined by every academic institution. It is an argument in itself guided by reasoning while showing the interrelatedness of the various parts within it following all rules of academic writing. You should always bear in mind that "Good

2. Hofstee, *Constructing a Good Dissertation*, 3.

academic writing is clear and concise, formal and precise."[3] These are aspects which a scientific research proposal is supposed to have.

WHY WRITE RESEARCH PROPOSAL?

There are several reasons for people engaging in writing research proposals. Three of them are the following: first, they are written in order for people or institutions to apply for grants in order to implement a certain project, e.g., an HIV/AIDS Education Project in villages. *Grantsmanship* is currently an industry whereby some people or organizations earn income through writing proposals and asking for funding from funding agencies. Nevertheless, grant providers cannot be willing to offer their financial assistance on the project which they do not know about. A well–written project proposal will convince grant providers that there is a valuable intervention planned out there which needs support. Therefore, a project proposal for a grant has to be as substantial as possible to convince grant providers on the importance and value of what is planned.[4]

Second, research proposal is written as an academic task in tertiary education institutions. Before students can go to collect data in order to write their dissertations, theses, or research papers, they have to write an acceptable research proposal. After acceptance, it becomes the basis for the data collection, analysis and report writing as a whole.[5] Moreover, it convinces evaluators about the competence of the student to execute a particular project, and becomes the basis for the relationship between students and their supervisors in the following research processes.

Third, it is written as a prerequisite for ones employment in certain research institutions. The sponsor needs to certify the proposed works which the applicant has proposed to do in that institution. In this case, the applicant will have to write a convincing research proposal in order to convince the employers of the outcomes of the proposed researches.

3. Hosftee, *Constructing a Good Dissertation*, 187.

4. Cf. Organization for Economic Co-operation and Development, *Promoting Research* (2014); Neuman, *Social Research*, 477–479.

5. Neuman, *Social Research*, 477.

MAJOR COMPONENTS OF GOOD RESEARCH PROPOSAL

In the beginning of this chapter we showed that the proposal is an academic or scientific document. As an academic document, a research proposal follows a specific pattern and has major components which comprise it that are academically acceptable. The components are the same in whatever proposal, whether it is just for a research paper that a student prepares in order to fulfill a certain course requirement, a thesis or dissertation for a particular degree to be evaluated by a committee in virtue of research for that degree, or a proposal to apply for funding of a particular project.[6] The contents for a Research Proposal should have the following obligatory key issues as broad topics in it: the Introduction, the Literature Review, the Methodology, the Data Presentation, analysis and Discussion, and the Conclusion. Though detailed components of research proposals may differ in arrangements and content depending on the discipline of study, and the type and purpose of research, some of the major components often included in a research proposal are the following, all reflecting the above-mentioned key issues:[7]

i. The Research title,

ii. Abstract,

iii. Introduction and background of research,

iv. Statement and significance of the research problem,

v. Research objectives,

vi. Theoretical background and literature review,

vii. Methodology and hypotheses,

viii. Implications and feedback

ix. Timetable of research implementation

x. References

xi. Budget

Therefore, in the following sub–sections we will discuss each of the components above in a more detail.

6. Ary, Jacobs, Sorensen & Walker, *Introduction to Research*, 607.

7. Silverman, *Doing Qualitative Research*, 188.

Research Title

As we discussed in the previous chapters of this book, the research title emanates from your research idea and should provide the whole of what readers expect to see in the research report. It tells the "what" of the research. Always the title should be shorter and clearer (my rule, not more that 20 words). It can be formulated as a one line title, e.g., *"The analysis of the Effects of the use of Computers in Njombe Region"* or it can be formulated in a Main and Half–Title form (colon title), e.g., *"The Use of Computers: An Analysis of Their effects within Njombe Region."*

Remember that the title is the first thing that readers of your proposal will see. So, it must be attractive, descriptive, and promising. It must be focused to one specific issue and concise. This means that the title must assure the reader that the research planned is researchable and worthy doing. Hence, in formulating your title avoid all unnecessary punctuations that will make your title obscure, e.g., commas, full stops, hyphens, etc.

Abstract

An abstract is primarily a short summary or a concise overview of what the proposal is all about which is always written at the end of the proposal writing. This part of the proposal is normally 100 to 150 words summary or overview of what is inside the proposal. In the abstract, you summarize the significance of research as a whole and the major contributions which your research will provide to the community. Hence, the abstract must be well–written and should reflect in an honest manner what is presented inside the proposal because the reader of the proposal can judge the worthiness of it through just reading the abstract. However, the abstract is written mostly in larger research projects that need larger proposals not in small ones.

Introduction and Background

This part of a research proposal sets a stage of the work presented in the whole proposal. It does three major things:

1. It states the background of the problem; where does it originate, how, and why. This assertion means that it states the magnitude of the problem as it is during the time you write your research proposal.

2. It explains the context of the study process.

3. It tells why the research will be important to you, to the community researched, to policy–makers, and to other researchers in the field. This means that you state the rationale for your study.

Therefore, the introduction and background part should state briefly what is lacking in current researches which you want to deal with. It means that it should state the knowledge gap and how you intend to fill in that gap. Or, it should state your experiences or observations regarding the problem that prompted you towards investigating it.[8]

Statement of the Problem and Its Significance

Statement of the problem is the most important part of the proposal. It comprises of at least five aspects:[9] first, it *describes the topic* basing on the magnitude of the problem. Second, it *states what problem* will be studied in the research process. Remember, the problem can be stated as a question or as a statement. The research problem must be clearly stated and easy to understand and identify it within the whole statement of the problem. The important things in your research problem are the following:

1. What problem do you want to study? This question must be answered clearly and with as simple language as possible. Here, you have to state the content of the problem you want to focus on in your research process.

2. Why is this problem important? Here you provide the reasons for choosing that kind of problem and not others.

3. Which variables do you want to examine (for quantitative researches). Variables show relationships. They should be clearly identified from the statement of the problem and presented in the form of thesis or hypothesis. Variables to be examined should relate to the content of the problem you stated.

Third, the statement of the problem *states the evidence* that justifies the research problem. Fourth, it *states the deficiency in evidence* that focuses to your intended research problem and the need for expanding past research. Fifth, it *states the audience* that will use the outcomes of your research.

8. Dawson, *Introduction to Research*, 58.
9. Cresswell, *Educational Research*, 73.

Therefore, a clearly stated statement of the problem tells readers about the significance of your whole research process, and lack of clear statement tells them about the unreliability and uselessness of the planned research.

Research Objectives

Research objectives tell about the goal which you want to achieve in the research process. Research objectives are of two types:

Main Objective—The main objective tells about the goal which the researcher wants to achieve in the whole research and is always only one. The main objective of the research should relate clearly to the problem which you want to deal with in your research and the main research question which you purport to answer.

Specific Objectives—These are small objectives that contribute to the main objective. They may be between two, three or more. They focus on specific issues within the main objective. These objectives should relate directly to specific or data collection questions you formulated.

Therefore, both Main and Specific Objectives must be clearly stated and should have a direct link with the problem of the whole research.

Literature Review and Theoretical Background

Literature review means that you have to read the works of other researchers who have dealt with the problem you intend to deal with, or similar to yours. The literature review done should handle at least the following important aspects:

1. What is already known about the problem stated? That is, what have other researchers already done? It explores the current state of knowledge about the issue being researched.

2. Is there anyone in the literature reviewed who has done exactly the same as the one which you intend to do or something that relates to it?

3. What critical evaluation do you provide to what has been done by other researchers about the problem?

4. What is the gap of research that needs to be filled? That is, what is not done by previous researchers, which you want to do in your research?

5. Where does your work fit in with regard to what other researchers' works done before, and why is it important that you do your work in light of where it fits in?[10]

In handling the aspects listed above, you just do two things in your literature review process: first, you present the researches done by other researchers and what they found out according to every theme you have selected to deal with in the literature review section, if you have arranged it thematically. Second, you discuss these findings while evaluating them in light of your own proposed research. Therefore, the two processes above allow you to immerse into the understanding and dialoging with other researchers and their findings instead of just using them to support your views.

However, our experience indicates that most students and researchers confuse between "presenting one's own views on a particular theme while supporting them with citations from other authors" and "presenting, discussing, and evaluating the findings of other researchers in light of one's proposed research." The first aspect, which most students opt to do in their literature reviews, is simple to accomplish; however, it is not literature review in its real sense. The second aspect, which most students hardly opt to do it is hard and time consuming; however, it is what entails literature review in its real sense. Therefore, literature review enables you to learn from what others have done, dialogue with their findings, evaluate them, and build your research on what is already known from those findings. It enables you not to repeat in your research what others have already done.

The literature review should be divided into at least two parts: the theoretical background part, and the empirical literature review part. In the theoretical background part, you review the broad literature in order to ascertain the theory or framework you will base your research, while in the empirical part you review the literature closely related to your work in order to discover what other scholars have researched in order to fill in the gap of what they have not done. Therefore, a research without a theoretical base is like a house without a foundation; and a research without knowledge of what others have done will lead to no knew knowledge about the issue being researched.

In reviewing the literature for a particular theoretical background, you can decide to use a particular theory in your research for the purpose of modifying it, refuting it, or formulating another alternative theory. Moreover, you can use this theory as a perspective or point of view in dealing

---

10. Cf. Silverman, *Doing Qualitative Research*, 349.

with your research problem. Hence, the literature review should clearly state which theoretical perspective you will use, and for what purpose.

In reviewing the literature for both theoretical background and empirical review, you must use the *most resent* literatures possible. Old literatures will provide old knowledge and lead to no new discoveries. Moreover, the literatures reviewed must be *relevant* to the problem of the proposed research. Be sure to document and cite all quoted materials. Failure to do that will be plagiarism, a serious academic offence. All cited materials must be listed in the list of Cited Works or References at the end of the proposal in alphabetical order. That is very important.

Research Methodology

What is "Research Methodology, and what Research Method is?" These two concepts are somehow confusing to most students and experienced researchers alike. Most of them have used the concept of method in theplace of methodology, and vice versa. On the one hand, the concept "methodology can be defined as a global style of thinking, 'a general approach to studying research topics' (. . .) or an 'overall research strategy'"[11] A methodology is a study (*logos*) about method. As a study about method, methodology has four main components: the fundamental cognitive mode, the theoretical perspective, the *ad hoc* procedures, tools, or stratagems (tricks) which you use to tackle your research problem, and the formal procedures or steps which you use in tackling the problem after selecting a particular cognitive mode.[12] The four aspects are important components of a methodology.

Giampietro Gobo asserts that "Every knowledge–gathering act is guided by at least one cognitive mode: we learn by *listening* (to the radio for example), *watching* (television for example), *reading* (a newspaper, magazine or book), *questioning* someone (for example a person under arrest or suspect), *talking* with someone, or with ourselves through *introspection*."[13] The above–mentioned modes are cognitive because they enhance learning through the use of God–given multisensory processes. This means that every methodology used is guided by one or more cognitive modes in order to enhance leaning to occur.

---

11. Gobo, *Doing Ethnography*, 18.

12. Ibid., 18–19.

13. Ibid.

Theoretical perspectives are assumptions about a particular reality. They are explanations about the nature of reality at the time you study the problem (paradigm or perspective): do you adopt a realist, constructivist, constructionist, relativist perspective, etc.[14]

A theoretical perspective has to do with what theoretical paradigm or perspective you select to adopt. A theoretical perspective also explains the task of science. What do you believe about the task of science? Is science a tool to provide explanations or descriptions of phenomena, to change the phenomena being investigated, or a tool for emancipation? Therefore, your methodology should have at least one particular conception about the role of science.[15]

A theoretical perspective also should have a particular conception about your role in a particular study process. Are you an objective instrument of research or active participant in the construction of reality being studied? A methodology should adopt one conception about your role depending on the cognitive mode adopted.[16]

The *ad hoc* procedures, tools, or stratagems (tricks) are neither formal nor learned in books or class. They emanate from your own accumulated experiences. These are the tricks of research which scientists have depending on the experience they have in their field, and they are sometimes documented in research reports in the form of papers or books. The methodology should encompass the stratagems of research in a particular cognitive mode selected.[17]

A formal procedural steps part of a particular research methodology tells us about the components of a particular research design you selected. It tells us about the research methods to be used in research process, samples, sample size, and sampling procedures, how data will be analyzed after collection, how reporting will be done, what ethical issues will be considered in using a particular chosen instrument of data collection, etc.[18]

The above–outlined components of a research methodology imply that research methodology is wider than a research method and in most cases depends on the cognitive mode which you select to use in your

---

14. Gobo, *Doing ethnography*, 19; cf. Mligo, *Doing Effective Fieldwork*, 24–25, 87–93.

15. Ibid, 19–20.

16. Ibid, 20.

17. Ibid., 21.

18. Page, Barton, Unger & Zappavigna, *Researching Language*, 50; Gobo, *Doing Ethnography*, 21.

research process.[19] Research methodology is a study (*logos*) of the way you will conduct your research process.

On the other hand, the concept "research method" refers to a technique, a tool or an instrument which you use in collecting or analyzing data during the research process. The technique, instrument, or tool for research is one of the components of your research methodology.[20] In empirical researches, we use observations, interviews, or questionnaires as instruments for collecting data (primary data). You can, however, decide to base your research on existing materials (e.g., books, journal articles, magazines, etc) and analyze them (content analysis) in your process of collecting data (secondary data). Moreover, you can decide to collect both empirical and existing data. In whatever the case, you have to state clearly the general methodology of your proposed research, including the techniques, instruments or tools you will use in your research process in order to collect and analyze data, and why use that instrument, or tool. Hence, methods, tools, techniques or instruments are always used within a particular methodology.

Policy Implications and Feedbacks

There are two things in this section of the research proposal. First, you should state what implications for policy makers will the research have? Here you state how the possible results will influence policy–makers in the society about the problem being dealt with. Second, how will feedbacks be sent to the community which research was conducted so that that community can benefit from the research you have done. You need to state the ways through which the feedbacks about the research results will be communicated back to the community for its consumption.

Timetable

A timetable is a scheduled series of events that will be done during the research process. It tells which activity will be done, when, and where. A well–formulated timetable for research will be a road map to lead you towards fulfilling the various tasks in that particular research. Therefore, the

---

19. Gobo, *Doing Ethnograph*, 21.
20. Page, Barton, Unger & Zappavigna, *Researching Language*, 50.

timetable needs to be realistic in terms of time for the activities scheduled and places allocated while keeping to the deadline of the research process.

Budget

A budget is a detailed description of all costs that will be incurred during the research process. You need to tell all minor things that will be used in the research and their costs. If it is travelling, the details of the travels and their expenses must be stipulated. If it is stationery, the details of all stationery equipments to be used in research must be stipulated. If it is food, the meals to be taken during research must be stipulated and their respective costs. At the end the total cost of the whole research must be indicated. The realistic budget with all necessary details will help you in your research process, and the research funding agencies to see the possibility of funding it, or evaluators in an academic institution to see its feasibility.

References

This is the last, but important, part of your proposal proper. After this part you can add some appendices, if necessary. References are materials used in the writing of the proposal. You cannot finish writing a scientific proposal document without using other researchers' works because all academic or scientific documents build on existing knowledge in order to produce new knowledge. All works used, whether published or unpublished, must be listed at the end of the proposal. The list must be made in alphabetical order of the authors' surnames following the conventions of documentation proposed by your funding agency or an academic institution which will evaluate it for your degree, e.g., APA Style, MLA Style, Turabian, Harvard Style, etc. Consider the following two examples:

APA Style:

Mligo, E.S. (2012). *Writing academic papers: A resource manual for Beginners in higher-learning institutions and colleges.* Eugene, OR.: Wipf and Stock, Resource.

MLA STYLE:

Mligo, Elia Shabani. *Writing Academic Papers: A Resource Manual for Beginners in Higher-learning Institutions and Colleges.* Eugene: Wipf and Stock, Resource, 2012.

REVISING YOUR PROPOSAL

After you have completed writing the proposal following all the above components vigorously, you will have done a great advance in your research plan. However, completing the first draft of the research proposal is not the final intervention towards an accepted research proposal. Peter Wood advises us with the following words regarding the work after the first draft:

> The major part of writing for most people lies not in creative composing [of research proposals], but in editing—re-writing, rephrasing, re-ordering, re-structuring, moving parts of the text around, adding to and deleting text, clarifying (. . .), removing ambiguities, sharpening, tightening, tidying up grammar, and so on. This is even more important in (. . .) research, since 'Discursive texts easily become wordy, run-on, repetitive, and redundant.'[21]

Wood's words above imply that when editing you should also meticulously re-read and re-write your research proposal after completing the first draft in order to make sure that most issues that lead to proposal rejection are fixed. This re-reading and re-writing is what it means by revising as Richards states it using Murray's words: "revision 'is re-seeing, re-thinking, re-saying, [while] editing . . . is making sure the facts are accurate, the words are spelled correctly, the rules of grammar and punctuation are followed.'"[22] Therefore, according to Richards above, editing is a component of revising and should not be taken separately.

What Makes Most Proposals be Rejected?

Many proposals for academic and grant application purposes have been rejected for various reasons related to editing and revising. Leedy and Ormrod highlight some of the issues that cause rejection of most research proposals as outlined below.[23]

21. Wood, *Successful Writing*, 81.
22. Murray in Richards, *Doing Academic Writing in Education*, 129.
23. Leedy & Ormrod, *Practical Research*, 234–235.

a) *Unclear statement of the problem*—check to ensure that your statement of the problem is stated clearly and can be well–understood by your readers. Moreover, it should clearly address the research area of your funding agency or academic institution you intend to submit. This is because an unclear statement of the problem is an obvious indicator of unclear proposal and unreliable research to be conducted.

b) *Incomplete methodology*—check to ensure that your methodology explains or stipulates how you will deal with the research problem you propose. An incomplete or unsatisfactory discussion of the methodology is a good indicator of your failure to reach the stated research goals. Therefore, make sure that your methodology describes in detail the way research will be carried out to reach your anticipated goal.

c) *General treatments of sub–problems is not clear*—check to ensure that your proposal clearly describes how the obtained research data will be used or interpreted in order to answer the questions for your sub–problems or the overall problem identified in your research proposal. Issues of how data will be presented and analyzed must be described in as detail as possible.

d) *Format of the proposal does not correspond with the academic institution*—check to ensure that the format of your proposal corresponds with the guidelines set forth by your academic institution or the funding agency where you intend to submit your research proposal.

e) *Inappropriate Citing of sources*—check to ensure that all cited sources for your proposal are correctly cited and all appear in the list of references at the end of the proposal. This means that the citations found in the text of the proposal should correspond with the list of references you provide. Make sure that the citation style you use is consistent and corresponds with a particular style accepted by your academic institution or funding agency (i.e., MLA, APA, Turabian, Harvard, etc)

f) *The research problem stated is not important and convincing*—check to ensure that your research problem is important and convincing to your academic institution or your funding agency. Academic institutions will not allow you to conduct research on unimportant research problem, and neither will funding agencies provide funding for such unworthy problem, a problem that is unlikely to yield new and interesting information.

g) *Lack of Focus*—check to ensure that the development of your proposal always focuses on the proposed research problem from the beginning to the end. A well–focused research proposal allows your academic institution or funding agency to be clear of the main agenda of your research.

h) *The researcher's unfamiliarity with the existing literature*—check to ensure that you have shown familiarity with current and relevant existing literature on which you locate your research work. Your literature review section and your use of other people's works to present your argument in the proposal should indicate this familiarity more clearly.

i) *Lack of clear statement on the researcher's adherence to ethical standards*—check to ensure that you have stated the possible ethical issues involved in your research proposed and how you will deal with them. A clear statement of how the integrity of informants, and how you will handle other people's researches should be provided clearly.

Therefore, the above–highlighted issues stand as reminders of some of the issues that a meticulous research proposal writer needs to take care of after completing the first draft.

What makes a Good and acceptable Research Proposal?

In the process of revising and editing your research proposal, you should pay attention to some important aspects that make a good and acceptable research proposal. Dawson lists them as follows:

1. A good research proposal has clear "Relevance, either to the work of the funding body or to the student's course."[24] By "relevance" it refers to the relationship between what you propose and what your funding agency or study course requires you to undertake. This means that what you propose should be directly related to what your funding agency requires or what your department would expect you to undertake in relation to what you are studying. Therefore, revise your proposal to ensure that it is relevant to your studies or the requirements of your funding agency.

2. In a good and acceptable proposal, "The research is unique, or offers new insight or development." Here "uniqueness" means providing

24. Dawson, *Introduction to Research*, 63.

something new that contributes to the existing knowledge. Uniqueness means breaking a new ground in the ongoing research about that problem in your field of study. Therefore, a good research proposal should clearly indicate what uniqueness it has in relation to the existing researches.

3. In a good and acceptable proposal, "The title, aims and objectives are all clear and succinct."[25] Revise to ensure clarity in your title, aims (or main objectives) and specific objectives stated. Ensure that your title is short, clear and to the point. Your main objective should clearly relate to your research problem, and the specific objectives should relate to your main objective.

4. In a good and acceptable proposal, "Comprehensive and thorough background research and literature review has been undertaken."[26] Be careful with the way you review your literature in a research proposal. It has to be as comprehensive as possible for your reviewers to be convinced that it provides adequate background to your research problem.

5. In a good and acceptable proposal, "There is a good match between the issues to be addressed and the approach being adopted."[27]

6. In a good and acceptable proposal, "The researcher demonstrates relevant background knowledge and/or experience."[28]

7. In a good and acceptable research proposal, the "Timetable, resources and budget have all been worked out thoroughly, with most eventualities covered."[29]

8. A good and acceptable research proposal has "Useful policy and practice implications."[30]

Therefore, if your proposal has been revised and edited to fit the above-listed qualities, it will be a good proposal worthy taking into account by your funding agency or course assignment providers in your department.

25. Ibid.
26. Ibid.
27. Ibid.
28. Ibid.
29. Ibid.
30. Ibid.

This means that as you construct your research proposal you are required to strive towards meeting the above-outlined criteria.

CONCLUSION

Indeed, it takes time and energy to write a good and convincing research proposal document with all the above–listed qualities. However, serious and committed students or researchers can see that meeting the above-listed criteria is part of fulfilling the ambitions to write well–crafted, well–thought, and well–checked research proposals. The words of Leedy and Ormrod summarize succinctly the overall quality of the carefully crafted, well–thought and meticulously checked proposal as they write: "A proposal for any research endeavor merits words that are carefully chosen, a style that is clear and concise, attention to the most minute procedural detail, and for each procedure, a rationale that is logically and clearly stated. All of this is a tall order, but the result reveals the scholarship of the proposal author as perhaps no other academic assignment can ever do."[31] In fact, we should emphasize that for a serious student and considerate researcher, this is quite possible by following the guidelines discussed in this chapter!

FURTHER READING LIST

Ary, Jacobs, Sorensen & Walker, *Introduction to Research in Education*, 606—634.
Organization for Economic Co–operation and Development. *Promoting Research* (2014).
Silverman, *Doing Qualitative Research*, 187–195.
Punch & Qancea, *Introduction to research Methods*, 2014:345–373.
Neuman, *Social Research Methods*, 477–479.

31. Leedy & Ormrod, *Practical Research*, 136.

Chapter 5

INSTRUMENTS FOR DATA COLLECTION

"In order to collect data, some form of measuring instrument has to be used. In the natural and health sciences, these would probably be sophisticated instruments ranging from high-resolution microscopes to gas spectrometers. In the human sciences, 'measuring instrument' refers to such instruments as questionnaires, observation schedules, interviewing schedules and psychological tests."

—Mouton, *How to Succeed*, 100

INTRODUCTION

AFTER YOUR PROPOSAL HAS BEEN ACCEPTED by your academic institution, your grant provider or your anticipated employer, you will now have to implement what you proposed in your proposal, according to your selected research design. You will have to use all the instruments you proposed in your research design to collect data in order to deal with your research problem.[1] Therefore this chapter defines research instrument, discusses the types of research instruments mostly used in social sciences and

---

1. Axelrod & Windell, *Dissertations Solutions*, 10.

the humanities (observation, interviews, and questionnaires), discusses the types of data collected by using those instruments, and the uses of the collected data.

WHAT IS DATA COLLECTION INSTRUMENT?

The question we first have to answer is this: What are research or data collection instruments? Research instruments include all techniques that enable you to collect data from the field or from any other place of study. You have two options here: you can either use the well–known existing instrument, or formulate your own.[2] In whatever the case, for the research report to be reliable, you need to use valid and reliable instruments for data collection. Research instruments are sometimes called methods, techniques, or tools for data collection and analysis.

TYPES OF INSTRUMENTS FOR DATA COLLECTION

As stated in the definition above, an instrument is primarily a tool used to enhance a particular task. In research, an instrument is a tool or technique, or method used in order to enhance the process of collecting research information to answer a particular research question. There are numerous research instruments. However, this book discusses only three major instruments commonly used in social sciences and the humanities.

Observation Method

The first instrument is *observation.* This is a research instrument you use to collect data to answer the research question for your research problem through making sense of what you see with your naked eyes. In this type of research technique you observe what goes on in the naturalistic or clinical setting and write notes on what has been observed.[3] Though this instrument may be used in quantitative researches (structured or systematic observation) to produce quantitative data for testing theories, in most cases, this instrument is used in qualitative research designs, e.g., ethnographic

2. Mouton, *How to Succeed,* 100.

3. Tomal, *Action Research,* 38–44; Angrosino, *Doing Ethnographical and Observational Research,* 54.

research design, where researchers subjectively explore lived experiences of people observed (unstructured observation). Therefore the main body organ responsible in this instrument is the trained eye and its ability to view what goes on in the study area and making commonsense judgments about it.

Observation has several advantages over interviews and question-naires. Some of them are the following:[4] first, it can be used to acquire re-search information from people who cannot speak or write for themselves, for example, children, and mentally and bodily disabled people. Second, you as researcher can obtain information in environments where you can-not access them using questionnaires and interviews, e.g., places where people are afraid of the consequences of your research, have no enough time to talk to you, or are not willing to participate in research through interviews and questionnaires. Third, observation may be the best way to access research information relating to behavior which participants can-not explain through interviews and questionnaires because they take it for granted. The trained eye of the observer may be able to ascertain the taken-for-granted behavior which would be difficult for them to explain. Fourth, the observer records firsthand information which does not depend on someone else as the writer or speaker. Fifth, observation can be used as a good supplement to other methods: interviews and questionnaires because it enables the acquisition of tacit data through the trained eye.

However, some disadvantages of observation are the following:[5] first, the environment can be inaccessible for the observers to see with their eyes what goes on. In such situations interviews or questionnaires are necessary. Second, it is possible for people to change their behavior when they discover that you observe them (*Hawthorne effect*). The way people will react to your presence as researcher is unpredictable. In this case, their negative reaction will cause your information to be an inaccurate representation of the actual behavior in their natural settings in the absence of the observer. Third, it is hard for any interpretation to provide the exact representation of the reality in the setting because any information provided is just a construction of the observers about the reality they see. This information is their interpreta-tion of that reality which may be different from their presentation. Fourth, observation consumes a lot of time and incurs much cost. This means that, you will have to spend a considerable amount of time in the environment

4. Foster, "Observational Research," 59–60.
5. Ibid.

to observe people's behavior and collect information in a limited number of behaviors.

There are three strategies of observation which you can use in your observation depending on the role you assume while in the field of study: participant observation, non-participant observation, and disguised observation. Let us discuss briefly each one of these strategies below.

Overt Participant Observation

In this strategy of the observation instrument your identity is fully known by those being observed and is done after their informed consent. You observe while participating partially or fully in what goes on within their setting. For example, you can participate in women activities in the society while observing the problems they encounter in what they do. In this kind of study you live with people you observe for a number of months (not less than six) or years, learn their language and culture, participate in their economic and social life, and negotiate your acceptance in that culture as an "insider." This negotiation will enable people who are observed to be free to show their behavior in a real sense.[6]

Non-Participant Observation

In this strategy of the observation instrument you just observe what goes on in people's natural settings without participating in what they do. For example, you may observe the way staff perform their duties, the way people interact, the way doctors treat patients, etc., without participating in what they do.[7]

Disguised Observation

This is the strategy of observation instrument in which the observer's presence or identity is totally not known or is partially known to the people/group he/she observes. The disguised observer may be participant or

6. Fraenkel, Warren & Hyun, *How to Design and Evaluate*, 446—447; Angrosino, *Doing Ethnographical and Observational Research*, 54—55; Casley & Lury, *Data Collection*, 69.

7. Fraenkel, Warren & Hyun, *How to Design and Evaluate*, 446—447; Angrosino, *Doing Ethnographical and Observational Research*, 54-55.

non–participant observer.[8] Giampietro Gobo distinguishes two kinds of disguises: first, the covert observation whereby the identity of the observer is fully not known by those being observed and no consent is sought before commencing the observation. The second is semi–covert observation whereby only a few of those being observed know the observer's identity while the majorities do not know him or her. Informed consent can be sought to those few who know the observer's identity, or not sought at all.[9]

The major problem with disguised observation is that it becomes suspect by the ethical standards of research, especially the obligation to obtain informed consent from informants before research and endorsement from research clearance bodies.

To repeat what we stated in the beginning of the discussion of this instrument, we emphasize here again that the major overall advantages of observation as an instrument of data collection, are the following: first, the researcher is the one who records the data concerning the physical world and the behaviors watched directly without relying on the accounts of others as it is in interviews and questionnaires. Second, the researcher is capable of "seeing" many things which are taken for granted by the participants in research. A trained eye of the researcher may uncover the strangeness of the various issues that people observed consider to be normal. Third, observation can provide information from environments and situations that cannot complete questionnaires or participate in interviews. For example, you as researcher can just watch how animal life is, how buildings look the way they look, and why young children behave the way they behave. Though these cannot take part in the interview or complete a questionnaire, yet the researcher can provide an account of them through observation. Fourth, data from observation can serve as a supplement to data obtained from other sources. Research involves all human senses. Data obtained from interviews may be supplemented by observations, especially when you as researcher watch the non–verbal communications which the informant portrays during the interview process.

Despite the disadvantages mentioned when beginning the discussion of this instrument above, we emphasize here again that the major disadvantages of observations are the following: first, some areas, behaviors and events are inaccessible for researchers to observe. Examples of inaccessible

8. Fraenkel, Warren & Hyun, *How to Design and Evaluate*, 446–447; Angrosino, *Doing Ethnographical and Observational Research*, 54.

9. Gobo, *Doing Ethnography*, 107–109.

areas, behaviors, and events include, but not limited to, the following: military areas where civilians are not allowed to enter, human sexual behavior, and events that happened in the past. It becomes very difficult to obtain observational data in such areas, behaviors, and events. Second, people change their behavior when they recognize that you observe them for research purposes. They may disguise their actions from the normal actions in their everyday life, when a person outside their lives (the researcher) intervenes their private situation, or adapt actions which they believe that you as researcher want. When this happens, the data obtained becomes inaccurate representations of their actual behavior. This behavior of altering of their actions from their normal everyday life because of the researcher being with them is called *Hawthorne Effect*. Here is where the issue of informed consent becomes very difficult. Do you have to ask for consent from participants before observation or not? Asking for consent causes them to change their behavior, and observing them without consent is an ethical misconduct. Third, observational data depend greatly on the skills and ability of the researcher. This means that the data obtained will mainly depend on the ability and biases of the researcher at that particular time of observation. Fourth, observation is time consuming and costly. The researcher needs to travel to the place of observation and spend a considerable time making sense of what is being observed in a particular area of study.

Capturing Research Information from Informants

In all types of observation discussed above, research information from informants can be captured by using note-taking and tape recording. These two ways need to be used together because in some types of observation the researcher will have more than two places to pay attention. For example, in participant observations where you will have to participates in the activities done by your informants and yet record the information from informants. Tape recording will help in collecting audio information while note- taking will help in collecting visual information. This means that you will have to write as much descriptive notes as possible regarding the behavior you observe, and tape record verbatim words spoken by informants in the field.

Interview Method

The second instrument is *Interview*. This is a method of collecting research data whereby you converse with the participant directly or indirectly. This research instrument involves the exchange of words by using sounds produced by the mouth. In this method, both you and your participant talk. You ask questions, and the participant answers. Therefore, interview, is an oral or verbal communication between you and the one being researched. The main body organ responsible here is the trained mouth and its ability to talk.

Interview as a Philosophy

Rubin, H.J. and Rubin, I.S. inform us that interview is more than just a skill for acquiring research information from people. Interview is also a philosophy, a way of understanding their world from their inner conscience. They write thus:

> interviewing is more than a set of skills, it is also a philosophy, an approach to learning. One element of this philosophy is that understanding is achieved by encouraging people to describe their worlds in their own terms. A second component of this philosophy is that interviewing involves a relationship between the interviewer and interviewee that imposes obligations on both sides. Third, this philosophy helps define what is interesting and what is ethical and helps provide standards the quality of the research, the humanity of the interviewing relationship, and the completeness and accuracy of the write–up.[10]

This means that knowledge is embodied in people's experiences and can be accessed through carefully asking questions and listening to their answers without you (the interviewer) dominating the interviewee and imposing your world to the interviewee.

Characteristics of Interview

Corbetta outlines several characteristics of interviews:[11] first, interviews are "elicited by the interviewer." This means that interviews differ from normal

10. Rubin, H.J. & Rubin, I.S., *Qualitative Interviewing*, 2.

11. Corbetta, *Social Research*, 264.

conversations between people. Though the participant observer can gain knowledge through the normal conversations in the area of observation, interviews are different from normal conversations. Interviews are special appointments that you make in order to focus your discussion with the interviewer on particular issues of your research interest. In this case, a normal conversation does not need a request to discuss; it is spontaneous. However, the interview is requested by the interviewer for the interviewer's research purposes.

Second, interviewees "are selected for interview on the bases of a systematic data-gathering plan." This means that the selection of interviewees depends sorely on their possible representations. The information gathered from the selected interviewees must be capable of being generalized to the larger population. In that case, the interviewees you select must be those whom you believe that they have adequate information to be generalized to the other members of that population.

Third, in interviews "a considerable number of subjects [informants] are interviewed." This means that in qualitative interviews the number of interviewees is relatively small using verbal communication. The number of interviewees for the interview process will be small because the goal of interviews is not quantities of interviewees but qualities of data obtained, not gathering information from people in order to test a particular relationship of concepts or variables, but to understand those people and their worldviews.

Fourth, an interview has a "cognitive objective." This means that interview seeks to understand the world of the interviewee by the use of spoken words through speaking to and hearing from the interviewee. It also involves the use of eye sight to see and make sense of the non-verbal communication from the interviewee, or to communicate information to the interviewee non–verbally.

Fifth, interview "is guided by the interviewer." Interview is not an aimless conversation between the two sides; rather, it is a process whereby you as researcher establish a particular conversational topic which will guide your conversations to ensure that your cognitive goals are fulfilled.

Sixth, interview "is based on a flexible, non–standardized pattern of questioning." This means that interview is different from a questionnaire. A questionnaire has rigidly predetermined questions expecting to acquire similar answers to all informants. Interview is flexible in both questioning and the responses anticipated from informants. Moreover, questionnaires are determined to collect information from respondents objectively while interview is determined to understand them subjectively.

The interview types

Some scholars divide interview into several types depending on style and focus of the interview: the topical oral history that focuses on a particular historical event, the life histories that focuses on the experiences of the interviewees in their various stages of life, evaluation interviews that focus on learning about the success or failures of particular programs, and focus groups that focus on hearing shared impressions about a particular phenomenon under study.[12] Therefore, interview is most favorable in qualitative research designs, e.g., phenomenological and ethnographic research designs, which focus on exploring people's cultures, worldviews, and experiences.

In this book we will discuss two major types of interviews basing on the ways the researcher has contact with the interviewee: the direct contact and telephone interviews.

Direct Contact Interviews

In this type of interviews data are collected through meeting the interviewee face-to-face and asking them questions. You ask questions and the interviewees respond to those questions. The eye-to-eye interview can be "individual" (the interviewee and the interviewer) or "focused group" interview (the group of interviewees and the interviewer). In both cases, the interviewer or researcher asks questions and the interviewees provide answers. The verbal answers provided and the nonverbal (tacit) communications (e.g., eye movements, body postures, hand gestures, facial expressions, and head movements) indicated by the respondent during the exchange of words are your data because all carry meaning with them.[13]

12. Cf. Rubin, H.J. & Rubin, I.S., *Qualitative Interviewing*, 26–28.
13. Gorden, *Basic Interviewing Skills*, 103.

Telephone Interview

In this type of interviews you and the interviewee are not together. You are far apart. The interviewer asks questions through telephone calls and the interviewee responds. The response of the interviewee is your data. This method is considered to be most effective because it minimizes time and costs for the interviewer to travel to the interviewees. The method also allows the interviewer to reach informants in whatever geographical places they are. However, some of its disadvantages include, but not limited to, the following: the inability to obtain tacit data (i.e., data generated via the informants' nonverbal communication), inability to reach people who do not have telephones, and the possibility for the interviewees to disconnect interview at any time during the interview process if not interested in the asked questions.[14]

Data CollectionQuestions in the Interview Process

Questions in the interview process may be closed or open–ended data collection questions. Closed data collectionquestions are the ones which informants are restricted to answering yes or no, or providing one particular anticipated answer. Both the questions and the response categories are determined by the interviewer before hand. The interviewee will have to select from among these categories during the interview process without adding anything more to the response categories predetermined by the interviewer. The advantages of closed questions are the following: easy analysis of data obtained, easy to compare among responses, and many questions can be asked within a short time. Their disadvantage is that respondents will have to fit their experiences, perceptions, and feelings to the response categories predetermined by the interviewer; otherwise, the interview process cannot be successful.

Open–ended data collection questions are questions that the informants are free to respond whatever they think. These questions are mostly used in qualitative interviews. The advantage of open-ended questions is that they reduce the interviewer bias shown in closed questions and enables adequate exploration of the interviewees experiences, perceptions, and feelings. Its disadvantage is that it may affect the interviewer's main

14. Panneersevam, *Research Methodology* (2012).

focus because the interviewee is free to explain oneself whatever aspect in response to the open–ended question asked by the interviewer.[15]

Moreover, questions in interviews may be *Structured, Semi–Structured, or unstructured* questions. By "structured questions" here we mean that you ask similar data collection questions with predetermined format and wording to all informants with the aim of obtaining similar information from all. This is also called a *standardized interview* whereby informants receive a similar treatment, i.e., you ask your interviewees the same data collection questions, in the same sequence. There is no freedom to inquire for further information from the interviewee, either by probing or follow–up, in this type of questions. You rely only on the data obtained from the structured questions you ask informants; and you assume that all informants will understand your questions in a similar way. However, this type of questions is more common in questionnaires, not in interviews. The advantage of structured questions is that since interviewees answer the same questions in the whole interview process, it is easy to compare responses from one interviewee and another during the analysis process. The disadvantage for it is that there is no flexibility to probe from the response provided by the interviewee.[16]

By Semi–Structured, or semi standardized, questions we mean that you ask similar predetermined data collection questions to all informants, but allow some freedom to probe behind a particular answer, prompt a discussion, or follow–up on issues asked.[17]

By unstructured questions we mean that you ask different not predetermined data collection questions to every informant with the aim of obtaining different information. This is called *non–standardized interview* whereby informants receive different treatments (cf. the last characteristic of interview above). The aim of these questions in the interview is to have in–depth exploration of the informants' experiences and interpretations of the world around them. These questions are always open–ended questions with a freedom to informants to respond and freedom to you as researcher to explore further by asking probing and follow–up questions.[18]

---

15. Patton, *Qualitative Research*, 349.

16. Patton, *Qualitative Research*, 349.

17. Punch & Quncea, *Introduction to Research*, 184; Rubin, H.J & Rubin I.S., *Qualitative Interviewing*, 5–6; Gorden, *Basic Interviewing Skills*, 145–165.

18. Ibid, 185; Rubin H.J. & Rubin, I.S., *Qualitative Interviewing*, 5—6.

Probing data collection questions are important in semi–structured and unstructured interviews because they provide a signal to the informant that you need more information about the question asked (the informant needs to keep on elaborating about the issue), that you seek more clarification from what the informant has just said, and that you pay attention to the ongoing interview process.[19] Therefore, as Rubin, H.J. and Rubin, I.S. summarize: "Probes clarify and complete the answers, making them intelligible, and signal the interviewees about the expected level of depth. They also show the interviewee that the interviewer is interested in the answers."[20] Probing questions are asked during the interview time, just after the data collection question is asked to the informant. Consider the following examples of probing questions:

1. This is interesting. Can you please elaborate more on it?

2. Yes, it sounds very good. Can you please clarify it more?

3. Oh God? Why do you think this is interesting?

4. I have not understood clearly. What do you mean by saying that?

5. Can you please elaborate further on this aspect?

Follow–up data collection questions explore further regarding the information which you obtained during the interview time. This means that follow–up data collection questions are usually prepared after the interview session and after reviewing the responses obtained and finding the need for more depth. Follow–up questions may base on the data collection questions asked during the interview time, a particular theme prompted by the interview done, or the general unclear context regarding what the informant provided in the interview time.[21]

Moreover, interview using unstructured questions can operate in two forms: first, as a guide interview whereby you arrange your questions in terms of topics or issues to be covered. These issues or topics are prepared in advance just for providing the interview its logic. The questions and their wording are obtained in the course of the interview process. The second is a conversational interview whereby you do not arrange questions in terms of topics or issues to be covered. Questions emerge spontaneously according to the topic of conversation, the context of conversation, and the course of

19. Rubin, H.J. & Rubin, I.S., *Qualitative Interviewing*, 148.

20. Ibid., 151.

21. Rubin, H.J. & Rubin, I.S., *Qualitative Interviewing*, 151.

setting. This means that there is neither questions, topics, nor wording of questions are prepared beforehand. In this case, everything depends sorely on the context of conversation.[22]

Capturing Research Information in Interviews

For better capturing of interview information, you require to use both note–taking and tape–recording strategies. This is because it will become difficult to you to pay attention to the interviewee by only using a note taking strategy. Interviewing needs that you always face your interviewee to see the nonverbal information communicated to you during the interview process and note it accordingly. It also requires you to listen carefully at the words spoken by your interviewee and note them verbatim. However, using tape–recording alone is inadequate because it will not record the non–verbal communication done by the interviewee. You have to use both strategies to enhance better capturing of interview research information.

In the interview process, note–taking will help you formulate probing questions and note the nonverbal information. This means that while the tape records the whole interview verbatim, the notes taken "will consist primarily of key phrases, list of major points made by the respondent, and key terms or words shown in quotation marks that capture the interviewee's own language."[23]

Questionnaire Method

The third Instrument we consider in this book is *Questionnaire*. In principle, a questionnaire is a set of questions from you which have been written and sent to the informants so that they can provide answers. The informant provides answers to the questions through writing and returning the written script to you. You can send questions to informants through printed papers (hard copies), fax, or e–mail (soft copies). Therefore, the main aim of questionnaires is not exploring in order to understand the informants' worldview, but gathering objective information from them.

In responding to the questionnaire, the informant has to struggle alone to understand what you have asked and respond to it accordingly. There is

22. Patton, *Qualitative Research*, 349.
23. Patton, *Qualitative Research*, 383.

nobody to clarify to what has been asked. Since the informant struggles alone to understand what you have asked, you have to ask as clear questions as possible in order to enable the informant understand them without problem. The main body organ responsible in this instrument is the trained hand and its ability to write your structured and predetermined data collection questions and alternative answers for the respondent to select.

Administering Questionnaires

Questionnaires can be administered through the following ways: first, it can be sent to the informant as a normal letter. When the informants receive it, they fill in and return to you as a normal letter. In order to succeed sending the questionnaires, you have to know the addresses of your informants. Moreover, you may send an empty envelop with a stamp in order for the informant to use after filling the questionnaire.

Second, it can be sent as a fax. In using this method, you write questions on a paper and fax them to the informant. You have to know the fax numbers of your informants in order to succeed in this method.

Third, it can be sent as an e-mail. The questions are written in an e-mail and sent to the e-mail address of the informant. It means that you have to know the e-mail addresses of your informants and must have a computer. The informants also must have computers in order to respond to your questions.

Fourth, it can be administered to a specific group of people. The group can be of teachers, of Information Technology Technicians, of administrators, of students, of officers, etc. You write questions on papers and distribute them to people who in turn answer them. You collect the papers as soon as they have finished answering. However, you must explain clearly the purpose of your research before the informants answer the questions.

Therefore, the administration of questionnaires suggests their advantages: easy to acquire information from many people for a short time, informants can fill questionnaires at their convenient time, easy analysis of data from close questions, greater anonymity and privacy to informants, and no interviewer bias because the informant responds to the question on paper alone.

The advantages highlighted above do not underestimate the disadvantages of this instrument: low quality of data obtained in terms of completeness and accuracy, low response rate of the questionnaires distributed, no follow up of responses provided, informants' inability to read and write, and inability to correct the informants' misunderstandings of the asked questions.[24]

Data Collection Questions in the Questionnaire

As it is to interviews, questions in the questionnaire may be closed or open-ended . Closed questions are the ones which the answers for them are predetermined. The informants are restricted to answering according to the predetermined answers: yes or no, day or night, noon or afternoon, etc. They do not need to add anything of their own. These are characteristic of quantitative data collection questions in questionnaires. Open-ended questions are questions that informants are free to write what they think. Such questions are characteristic of qualitative questionnaires.[25]

Moreover, questions in questionnaires may be Structured, Semi-Structured, or unstructured data collection questions. By 'structured data collection questions' here we mean that you ask similar predetermined questions to all informants with the aim of obtaining similar information from all. By Semi-structured questions we mean that you ask similar pre-determined questions to all informants, but allow some freedom to informants to explain further about a particular answer within the questionnaire according to their own understanding. By unstructured questions you ask different questions to every informant with the aim of obtaining different information and informants have freedom to explain what they know about the issue asked.[26] Therefore, in the questionnaire freedom is only to the informant; you have no freedom to probe behind the informants' responses beyond the questions stipulated in the questionnaire sheet. However, you can have follow-up questions with another questionnaire after administering the first session and assessing the informants' responses. Moreover, since most questionnaires are used in quantitative research designs to test variables, they are mostly structured and closed ones.

24. Gillham, *Developing a Questionnaire*, 5–7.

25. Gillham, *Developing a Questionnaire*, 4–5; Koul, *Methodology of Educational Research*, 147.

26. Peterson, *Constructing Effective Questionnaires*, 29–44; Koul, *Methodology of Educational Research*, 147–148.

Covering Letter

A covering letter is an important document to be sent to the informant with the questionnaire. A covering letter must state clearly the following aspects:

a) The institution where you come from.

b) The major objectives of the research you intend to conduct.

c) The importance of the research conducted both to you and to the community at large.

d) The way the informant has to answer the questions enclosed.

e) The statement of freedom to participate in research or not. This means that the informant does not need to be coerced in any way in order to provide research information.

f) The statement to ensure confidentiality to all answers provided by respondents.

g) Your telephone numbers and your addresses for communication and for returning the questionnaires.

All the three instruments for data collection discussed above are concerned with the generation of data through your initiatives. Your skills to administer the methods discussed above greatly determine the quality of data generated. In this case, you are the "primary instrument" of research because you are the major determinant of the nature and quality of data generated.[27]

RESEARCH DATA

As stated above, the sole concern of any research is to collect data for a particular purpose by using acceptable instruments (methods, techniques or tools). This sub–section discusses about the data obtained after administering your research: what are they, their types, their sources, and their uses in regard to your proposed research problem. Therefore, this section demonstrates that data and their quality are the important factors in producing a satisfactory or unsatisfactory evidence for your argument for or against a proposed research thesis.

---

27. See Mligo, *Doing Effective Fieldwork*, 122–124.

What is Data?

Research scholar Hofstee states thus:

> In order to solve the problem you have set yourself—that is, to test your thesis about the problem you have identified in the form of a [research report],—you need to support your work with arguments. The quality of your work depends on the quality of the arguments you make. Arguments, in the academic sense, are not arguments unless you have evidence. In academics, no argument is stronger than the evidence for it—and evidence relies on data, and data comes from research.[28]

As Hofstee asserts above, data are materials (information) collected and organized for analysis for research purposes. This means that data come from research information; and Research information are materials that are just collected from the study but not organized for analysis. Therefore, data are any raw, unprocessed materials in the form of symbols, words, figures, numerals, etc, collected from the source and organized for analysis in order to serve a particular research purpose. For example, a set of returned questionnaires, tape recordings or notes of interviews, notes from documents, notes from observations, etc., are research information that need to be organized for analysis to serve your research purpose. In quantitative research data organization involves the systematic coding of the information from questionnaires in order to get a data matrix. This means that unless are analyzed and interpreted to serve your purpose, data are just a cluster of useless information.[29] The collection of these raw, unprocessed materials (information) (which are eventually organized for analysis) is done by using the above–discussed research methods: observation, interview, and questionnaire; or, through reading secondary sources.

Types of Data

There are two types of data depending on the approach which you select for your research—qualitative and quantitative data. On the one hand, qualitative data are data expressed in terms of words, figures, colors, etc., but not numbers. They are always descriptive found in three major forms: verbatim quotations of descriptions of people's feelings, perceptions, experiences,

28. Hofstee, *Constructing a Good Dissertation*, 51.
29. Cf. Punch & Qancea, *Introduction to Research*, 111.

notes descriptions of activities, interpersonal interactions, behaviors, actions, conversations, and whatever you observe, hear,and photograph from the field of study and excerpts and paraphrases from written and knowledge from interviews; detailed field

documents as a result of their content analysis.[30] "Documents the subjects [informants] write themselves or are written about them such as autobiographies, personal letters, diaries, memos, minutes from meetings, newsletters, policy documents, proposals, codes of ethics, statements of philosophy, yearbooks, news release, scrapbooks, letters to the editor, 'Dear Abby' letters, newspaper articles, personal files, and (. . .) case records and folders are included in the data."[31] On the other hand, Quantitative data are data in terms of quantity expressed by using numbers or numerals. Such data may be number of employees, number of People Living with HIV/ AIDS, number of poor people, etc.

Therefore, Patton expresses clearly the difference between quantitative and qualitative data, "quantitative data are systematic, standardized, and easily presented in a short space. In contrast, the qualitative findings are longer, more detailed, and variable in content (. . .)."[32] Following the difference stated above,, quantitative data are easy to analyze because they are systematic and aggregated together; while qualitative data are difficult to analyze because they are not systematic and aggregated together. Responses of people are in most cases random and informal in qualitative researches. However, both types of data can be obtained from different sources and by using different instruments of data collection.

Sources of Data

What are sources of data? Sources of data are places where you will obtain the information you need in order to answer your problem. There are two types of sources for data collection: primary and secondary sources. A primary source of data provides data called *Primary Data*. Primary data are raw materials that are not used anywhere else. These are data that you collect for the first time from the source, e.g., interviews, meeting minutes, etc, and use them in your research for the first time.

---

30. Patton, *Qualitative Research*, 4.

31. Bogdan & Biklen, *Qualitative Research*, 133.

32. Patton, *Qualitative Research*, 20.

Secondary source of data provides data called *Secondary Data*. Secondary data are raw materials that you use for the second, third, or more times. These are data that were collected and used by someone else, and you decide to use them again in your research. For example, data from books, from journal articles, from newspapers, from conference papers, and from magazines. This type of data was collected by other researchers and used by them for their own research purposes. They are raw materials to you because you will need to analyze present and interpret again to suit your research purpose. Therefore, the source of data mainly depends on the type of data that you want to collect. If you need primary data, you will use primary sources of data collection. If you need secondary data, you will use secondary sources of data collection.

Uses of Data

Why do we collect data? This is the primary question to answer when we want to consider about the uses of data. As we said in the previous discussions, the main purpose of research is to answer questions, solve problems, verify or construct theories. You cannot answer the research question without data. You cannot solve problems existing in societies without having adequate data regarding those problems. You cannot construct a theory about a certain existing phenomenon without data about that phenomenon. You cannot verify the validity of a particular theory without collecting data to disprove or prove the validity of that theory. Therefore, research information are collected and organized into data for a purpose; they are used as evidences of what you want to argue or wants to do in regard to a particular issue after they are processed (analyzed and interpreted).

CONCLUSION

This chapter was about the tools to help you execute research. We have introduced you to important research tools or techniques used in social sciences and the humanities: observations, interviews, and questionnaires. The chapter has demonstrated that a properly selected tool for research increases the reliability of the data obtained and the strength of the evidence to support your arguments in the research report. The type of question you design to ask, the careful attendance to the non–verbal communication in the interviews and observations are important aspects of data collection.

The type and execution of questionnaires also increases the success of the research process. Therefore, the success, validity, and reliability of data in a particular research intervention do not only depend on the technique you use in your research, but also on the way you design and execute it.

FURTHER READING LIST:

Mligo, *Jifunze Utafiti*, 37–72.
Kumar, *Research Methodology*, 119–123.
Upgade & Shede, *Research Methodology*, 46–69.
Panneerselvam, *Research Methodology*, 17–31.
Taylor, Sinha & Ghoshal, *Research Methodology*, 75–86.
Peterson, *Constructing effective Questionnaires*, 13–44.
Gorden, *Basic Interviewing Skills* (1992).
Casley & Lury, *Data Collection in Developing Countries*, Second Edition, 64–73.
Gillham, *Developing a Questionnaire*, Second Edition, 5–14, 45–48.
Angrosino, *Doing Ethnographical and Observational Research*, 43–58.

Chapter 6

WRITING RESEARCH REPORT

"Ultimately, what you put on paper and how you put it there reveals your knowledge, the quality of your thinking, and your standards of excellence more eloquently than anything else you do."

—**Leedy & Ormrod**, *Practical Research*, **324**

INTRODUCTION

STRICTLY SPEAKING, there is no formal research without a formal report! At the end of your research effort, you will have to communicate the knowledge gained to other readers. This is the most exiting stage of the research intervention because it presents the knowledge and the whole of your thinking about your problem of research. Therefore, strictly speaking, research report and the way you craft it presents your whole academic personality!

Leedy and Ormrod assert that the research report concerns four main things: First, "It should give readers a clear understanding of the research problem and why it merited an in-depth investigation."[1] Second, "It

---

1. Leedy & Ormrod, *Practical Research*, 325.

should describe exactly how data were collected in an attempt to resolve the problem."[2] Third, "It should present the obtained data precisely and completely."[3] Fourth, "It should interpret the data for the reader and demonstrate exactly how the data resolve the problem."[4]

In the following paragraphs we present the components of the final research report by looking at the four issues mentioned above in a more detail. We discuss what the preliminary pages of the report are all about, what each chapter of the report needs to cover, what constitutes the bibliography or references (Cited Works) of the report, and the editing of the report to finalize the work before we eventually look back to the main rules of the academic game in the final chapter of the book.

COMPONENTS OF RESEARCH REPORT

The research report as it stands is only one argument with small sub-arguments in it. Normally, the argument of the research report contains the following three components: preliminary pages, main body (with references), and appendices. We will discuss each of the three aspects in a more detail below.

Preliminary pages

Preliminary pages are pages that come before the "Introduction" chapter of your research report. Their main function is to guide the reader about the type of report, type of people you interacted with in order to produce the report, types of figures and tables included, key terms used in the report, and the executive summary of the whole report work. Preliminary pages are often written in lower Roman numbers. These pages are as important as the other parts of the report because they appear at the very beginning of the report. Therefore, they need to be well-stated and arranged in order to persuade the reader towards delving into the innermost part of the report.

The number of aspects in the preliminary pages always depends on the instructions of the discipline and institution where you do research. Normally, the preliminary pages part has the following components

2. Ibid.
3. Ibid.
4. Ibid.

arranged according to the sequence they should appear: first, the *Title Page*. The title page provides the reader with the first impression of what is inside the work. The title page has the name of the institution where the report is submitted, the title of the report (main and sub–title if necessary), full name of the author of the report (first, second and surname), the purpose for which the report is submitted (the requirement which the report fulfills), city and country, and date of submission (month and year). The title page is always page number "i" of the report. However, the page number is always suppressed, i.e., it is not visibly written.

The title of the report is the most important aspect in this page. It should be well–formulated, focused, concise, and descriptive reflecting the whole of what you have presented in the report, especially the research problem you have dealt with. Most researchers prefer to put participles in the main title of the research. For example, "*Deciding on the Real Cause: HIV and AIDS effects upon Youth in Tanzania.*" This makes the title live, practical, and reflects the characteristics of a good title containing the what, how, and who questions in it. Other researchers do not prefer to put participles in their main titles. For example, "*The Real Cause: HIV and AIDS effects among Youth in Tanzania.*" Both ways are convenient. What is important is that the title is focused, concise, and well–formulated for your readers to grasp what is presented inside the research report.[5]

The second aspect is the *Declaration Page*. In this page you provide an oath and confirmation that the report presented is your own work, and that it has not been presented anywhere else in part or in whole for the same or another purpose. Moreover, make an oath that the whole work presented is your own work except for the materials borrowed from other authors which you have duly acknowledged following an acceptable convention. Hence, in this page you declare responsibility to the work you have presented.

The third aspect is the *Acknowledgements Page*. This page expresses your sincere gratitude to the various people who have facilitated the success of your research work and report writing in one way or another. This is an important page because a curious reader may assess the credibility of your research and your report by just looking at the type of people who were involved in the research and report writing process. You may acknowledge the librarians, your supervisor, your funding agency, your institution, professors and fellow researchers who commented on your research

---

5. Cf. Silverman, *Doing Qualitative Research*, 333–334.

work, your informants, etc. Consider the following example statements of acknowledgement:

1. Your colleagues

   I am indebted to my classmates . . . , . . . , . . . , and . . . for reading and commenting on my research report. Their comments and suggestions are invaluable.

2. Your Supervisor(s)

   A vote of thanks goes to . . . who supervised my field and library research processes and the professional writing of the research report.

3. Your Financial Supporters

   This research work could not be realized without the auspice of . . . I owe a word of gratitude to them for their financial support.

4. Your Sources of information and disclaimer statement

   This work is a result of my (library, or fieldwork). I recognize the contribution of . . . in helping me obtain the information necessary to answer my research problem. However, none of the sources is responsible for the ideas expressed in this report. Of course, the responsibility for this report remains mine.

5. Your Family

   I convey heartily thanks to my wife/husband . . . for understanding my concerns during the research and report writing process. His or her words of encouragements were invaluable.

6. To your Deity

   I am grateful to Almighty God who sustained my life and guided me throughout this research. It is true that without God everything could not have been the way it is.

Remember that research is not a monopoly of a single person. Since research is not a monopoly of a single knowledgeable person, you need to ensure that the research and report writing process incorporates other experts in the relevant fields where your research falls in. Though you will not let other people write research for you, still you will need to obtain some ideas from as many people as possible in order to accomplish your report. The acknowledgements indicate your appreciation of all those who have made your research successful. Therefore, this counts for the reasons why should you acknowledge the contribution of others in accomplishing this noble research task.

The fourth aspect is the *Table of Contents Page*. This page presents the logic of your argument in the whole research report. The table of contents is presented in the form of brief words of chapters and sub–chapters including the page numbers where they will be found. The table of contents helps readers locate parts of your argument which they are of interest. Therefore, the table of contents needs to be logical, user–friendly, informative, and well–arranged because it shows how you are logical and capable of writing a well–presented argument of your report.[6]

The fifth aspect is the *List of Tables Page*. Tables are part of your research report, especially in your quantitative research. Tables convey a great deal of accurate numerical information. This page lists the tables you have included in the Main Body of your work in order to present data you obtained in the research including their subsequent pages where they are found. They should be numbered consecutively from the first table to the last one. Tables should contain two aspects: labels and titles. The label contains the word "Table" (not italicized) and the Arabic numeral of the table in the sequence of tables within the report. Both of them are written at the top of the table flush from the left hand margin. The title of the table and a brief explanation of what is the content of the table; it is double spaced and appears just below the label. The first letters of all principal words are capitalized and the title as a whole should be italicized. Consider the following examples of label and title in the Table.

Table 8
Occurrence of pregnancies among university students as freedom to interact with male students increases

The sixth page is the *List of Figures Page*. Figures are important aspects of your research report. In this page you list all the figures you used in the main body of the report to illustrate your arguments and their subsequent pages where they are found. The figures in this page include, but not limited to, the following: diagrams, pie charts (circular diagrams to show divisions and proportions), bar charts (to show trends and variations), maps, graphs (to show accurate information and trends), pictures, and printed music included in your report in order to illustrate a certain point.[7] Figures are arranged consecutively from the first to the last figure. As is the table, the

---

6. Cf. Silverman, *Doing Qualitative Research*, 337.

7. Emden & Easteal, *Report Writing* (1987).

figure also contains two aspects: the label and the caption double spaced if long. The label has the word "Figure" and the number of the label in the sequence of figures in the report both typed flush from the left hand margin below the figure and italicized. The caption provides explanations about the figure and is placed just after the label, not italicized. In that case, the caption serves as the title of the figure. Consider the following example of Label and Caption:

Figure 3. The Relationship between Student Monitoring and Class Performance.

As you can see in the example above, the number of the label is punctuated with a period before the caption, and the caption ends with a period. If the figure is taken from a certain source, you will need to indicate that source just after the caption. However, such a source will not necessarily appear in the references list.

The seventh aspect is the *Definition of Key Terms and Concepts* used in the study. We mention here "key terms and concepts" to imply that not all terms and concepts used in the study will need a definition in the beginning of the report. You will have to be clear of what are the key terms and concepts used in the research report. For example, the variables of your hypothesis or thesis you have tested, and the theories and models you have used will have to be defined. In order for readers to be aware of them you will have to define them at the outset for clarity.[8] However, in some researches key terms and concepts are defined in the introduction chapter of the report. In whatever the case, the definition of key terms provides clarity to readers as they continue reading the report.

The eighth aspect is the *Abstract Page.* The abstract covers the following five issues: what is your research problem (state the variables of the hypothesis or thesis you tested), why is that problem important and worth studying, your data and methods used to collect them, your main findings after presentation analysis and interpretation of the data, and the implications which the findings have in light of your research and other researches. These issues seem too many; however, the abstract has a limit of words. In most research reports the abstract has less than one hundred words. This assertion means that you have to say as many things as possible in as few

8. Cf. Silverman, *Doing Qualitative Research,* 336.

words as possible, using the present tense. That is one of the sole characters of a lively and informative abstract.[9]

Swales and Feak provide two approaches that you can use in writing a convincing abstract: the *result–driven* and the *summary–driven* abstracts. On the one hand, the result-driven abstract "concentrates on the research findings and what might be concluded from them."[10] On the other hand, the summary–driven abstract concentrates on providing a synopsis of what you have presented in the research report. In whatever the approach used, the abstract aims at being informative (including the findings of the research) not just being indicative (providing a brief description of the subject of the report without including the findings).[11] Moreover, if your research based on a particular theory or model, you will have to mention the theory or model onto which your research was based and how the findings correlate with the theoretical framework you used. Therefore when writing your abstract show the *motivation* for doing research, the research focus, the methods used in your research, the findings obtained and the conclusions reached. Your abstract should be only one paragraph, not more than 300 words, should contain all the mentioned aspects, and italicized. Consider the following example of the result–driven (informative) abstract below:

> [Motivation for research] *In recent years, there has been a growing interest among sociologists towards searching for the effects of stigmatization to social relations, especially in work places. Despite the various initiatives developed among agencies and organizations to deal with it, stigmatization remains a threatening phenomenon.* [Research focus] *This study focused on exploring the causes of the prevalence of stigmatization of People Living with HIV and AIDS (PLWHA) in church related organizations and the effects stigmatization has to the effectiveness of work in such organizations.* [Research method] *In order to meet this focus, the survey of various literatures on stigmatization was done in order to ascertain what is already known about it. This literature survey was followed by face-to-face individual interviews conducted to PLWHA and their colleagues at work in order to ascertain their experiences and the possible reasons for the persistence of stigmatization.* [Research findings] *Several outcomes of the research were vivid: first, living*

9. Ibid., 334.

10. Swales & Feak, *Academic Writing*, 282.

11. Swales & Feak, *Academic Writing*, 282.

> with HIV was equated with having a contagion that could con-
> taminate other people. Second, living with HIV was something to
> fear because a person of this category had a living- dead status and
> was equated with death itself. Third, living with HIV was equated
> with being less than being a human being. All these aspects were
> enshrined in the assumptions and beliefs of religious people in regard
> to contracting HIV which ultimately reduced the working morale of
> PLWHA when enacted towards them. [Conclusion] *In this case, the
> study concluded that the stigmatization of PLWHA at work within
> religious organizations is based on mere beliefs and constructions
> of humanity, and not on scientific bases.* [Recommendation] *This
> study recommends that serious policies that promote equality among
> workers in religious organizations regardless of one's heath status be
> formulated to curb the stigmatizing attitudes exerted to PLWHA by
> some fellow workers.*

The abstract presented above contains all aspects that constitute a well-written abstract. The important thing in writing the abstract is that it should come directly from what you have written in your research report. That is why it should be written after completing the whole report.

The Introduction Chapter

After looking at some of the aspects of the preliminary pages and under-standing what they present, readers of the research report will be interested to know about *what* you dealt with in your entire research report. Hence, you have to introduce that which you have dealt with. This means that in the introduction you tell your readers what you intend to tell them. You tell your readers the context of the problem. You tell them what goes on in that context that you think it to be a problem and in which way you think it to be a problem. This part of the report has to be concise and clear because it is the one that will lead readers into understanding the problem you state to them.[12] The introduction of your report begins with the first Arabic number.

In the introduction, you clearly state the problem you intend to in-vestigate in only one sentence or two. The problem for your research is within the topic you formulated earlier. You should always remember that no problem no research; and hence, no new knowledge will be generated, and no advancement in whatever angle. People will remain with the same

12. Cf. Silverman, *Doing Qualitative Research*, 337–339.

understanding of the world around. Therefore, problems are the foundations of science.

In your problem several other issues must be elaborated in order to clarify it to your readers: What exactly is the problem you investigated? Why do you think it to be a problem? What facets are there to it? Are there any efforts done before to address it? What are they? Have these efforts been successful or not? These questions should be clearly answered in order to make the problem statement clearly understood by your readers.

You clearly state the main research question which you address in the whole of your research work. The research question you state has to be a sport light to investigating your thesis statement. The research question should not contradict with the thesis statement; but it should show a relationship to it. This means that it should emanate from it. You also have to formulate specific research questions that will help test the thesis (hypothesis) statement.

You also clearly state what exactly do you want to achieve in your investigation. This means that you have to state the objectives for your research and offer explanations for everyone in order to make your readers understand what you want to achieve for every objective you mention. At the conclusion of your research report readers will assess if the objectives you stated have been achieved or not. This means that you need to make sure that the objectives you state in the introduction match with the outcomes of your research. The objectives statements usually start with "To . . ." followed by a verb "examine, investigate, evaluate, establish, prove, disprove, search, demonstrate, etc" (see Appendix C for more verbs)

State the thesis statement clearly and precisely. It is important that your readers understand it because it tells exactly what your study will investigate. This means that the investigation of the thesis will clearly tell exactly what research problem you identified because the two are interrelated. Moreover, the investigation of the thesis statement will directly lead to achieving the objectives you stated. The three aspects, research problem, research objectives, and research thesis, are interrelated. Therefore, in stating the thesis statement we usually say, "In light of the above (your problem and objectives you stated before), the thesis of this study is . . . " Then elaborate this thesis more as to why it is important to investigate its variables.

Tell your readers the delineation of your study. Here you tell what you will be responsible for in the report in regard to the thesis statement you investigate, and what is out of it that you are not responsible for. This will make you avoid criticisms from readers because the delineations limit the scope of your report.

You tell the limitations of your research and your report, what your research does not do and why, where were you not perfect in doing (weaknesses) and why, where are your conclusions limited and why. In stating the limitations and delineations we usually start with sentences such as, "This study will not deal with . . . " or "This research report will not consider . . ." followed by reasons for not doing that. Therefore, you have to name the limitations of your work because every work has them whether named or not, and readers will address them as they read. Naming and explaining them will reduce possible criticisms from your readers. Readers will know quite well that most of your limitations will not be deliberate but a result of restrictions in your ability to investigate your thesis: from the data or finance you were not able to obtain, from the time that was allocated for research, etc. These are methodological restrictions that will also have to be discussed in detail in the methodological chapter.

Provide definitions of specific terminologies as will be used in your research report. You should define words, terms, or concepts at the very beginning for readers to have the first impression of them before they see them inside the work. However, you have to stick to those definitions throughout your research report. Definitions may be yours, from a certain scholar, or from a dictionary. What matters is that you stick to them throughout your report. A scholarly written list of definitions of terms makes it simple for readers to refer when they have forgotten the meaning of a particular terminology, which would be a difficult task for them if the meaning of such terminologies were included in the main text.

Outline the assumptions you have about the thesis statement you investigate. They are just your assumptions. The report will still be strong for having strong evidence for what could be stated as assumption. In that case, it will be of no use stating the assumptions, but presenting the evidence of the research.

State the significance of your whole research; and state why your study is worth doing. The study must have a theoretical and/or practical significance. By theoretical significance we mean that you have to state how it will offer a new explanation of a particular phenomenon being investigated, or extends, redefines, or contrasts the existing explanation. By practical significance we mean how the study will be of benefit to you, to other scholars of your own field, to policy-makers, and to the community being researched towards solving an immediate problem. The literature review chapter will justify the statement of significance you state here.

Clearly state the anticipated audience of your report. As Michael Alley reminds us: "No matter what document you are writing, you should assess the audience: (1) who will read the document, (2) what do they know about the subject, (3) why will they read the document, and (4) how will they read the document."[13] This means that you have to outline the categories of readers for your report, assess the knowledge which your audience has about what you have written, the information which your audience need, and the possible way which your audience will use in reading your document to meet their purposes.

Eventually, state the chapter overview of your report. The chapter overview provides the layout of your arguments in chapters, subchapters and paragraphs. Therefore, you need to provide the way chapters are arranged and the main points which they posit. This will provide to the readers the logic of your main argument of your report, which is also found in the table of contents in a nutshell.

Generally speaking, the introduction chapter commits you and your promises to your readers. That is why we suggest that it should be written last. You become responsible for various promises and claims you make at the introduction: the definition of terms provided, the thesis statement to be tested or argued, the objectives to be achieved, and the research question to be answered in the investigation of the thesis. Since this section is so important, you must make sure that it is well–written from the proposal stage (because most part of the introduction will be found in the proposal) to the final report. It means that what you promise readers should be exactly what you plan to tell them in the body of the report. Therefore, there must be clarity of words and thoughts for readers to understand it well.[14] Clarity has to do with avoiding in all costs saying things that you do not mean by avoiding needless complexities in wording, phrases and sentences, and avoiding ambiguity in words, phrases, and sentences used to describe a certain matter.

---

13. Alley, *The Craft of Scientific Writing*, 5.

14. Cf. Leedy & Ormrod, *Practical Research*, 326; Moore, *How to do Research*, 131–132.

The Literature Review Chapter

After knowing the thing which you have dealt with in the introduction, readers will need to understand the type of literatures which you have reviewed to assess the current state of knowledge about the stated research problem. They will be interested to see the rationale for selecting that type of literatures and whether the review has been done appropriately in regard to what you dealt with in your research. After they have understood that your literature review is appropriate and uses relevant, prominent, and recent literatures, they will be convinced to believe that your study was worth doing. This is because they will clearly see the of gap research worth filling in the literature review.[15]

The literature review chapter is a crucial one in academic writing. It usually comes after the introduction and before the method chapters. Why is it that way? This is because you have told the readers in the introduction what you will do, and they have understood it. Now you have to show to them how you locate it in the relevant, prominent, and current secondary literatures. When we speak of "secondary literatures," we just mean the researches previously published by other scholars in your own field. You will have to review a few *prominent, recent,* and *relevant* literatures only. This is very important!

Remember that a good literature review has three characteristics: it should be *comprehensive* (providing all necessary information needed to know), *critical* (providing careful evaluation and judgment), and *contextualized* (well-placed in the secondary literatures). This means that it must provide a theory base of the work, a critical survey of the recently published works about the problem under investigation and provide an analysis of those works with critical evaluation and judgments about them.

As we have said above, the literature review chapter is an extremely important one; however, it is the one which every lazy student or researcher will not take into account because it involves much reading work. This chapter is important for at least five aspects: first, it measures your awareness of what goes on in regard to what you researched and your credentials. Readers will believe in what you have done after they believe that you have read extensively about it, and that you have situated it in the broad understanding of the published literatures. Your credentials (i.e., your being scholarly) will be measured on the way you handle the literatures of other

15. Cf. Silverman, *Doing Qualitative Research,* 340–350.

scholars: the way you select them, the way you organize them in the way that makes sense, the way you discuss them objectively, and the way you focus on the main issue of your research in the review process.

G. Marx clearly writes thus about how other scholars measure your credentials as scholar: "Even producers of literature must know literature, and a major criterion for evaluating work is whether or not it is put in a context of prior scholarship. We are not only creators of new knowledge, but also protectors and transmitters of old knowledge. Our inheritance is the astounding richness of the work of prior scholars."[16] These words mean that you cannot produce new knowledge from the air. New knowledge emanates from your ability to read other researchers' literatures diligently and making sense of them.

Second, literature review shows that your intended work is based on an existing theory. You cannot do any research work from the air. After all, you are not the only scholar in your field of study, though you might be the only person to deal with that particular problem. You have to show clearly the relationship of your research work to a particular existing theory. You have to relate your work to existing logical explanations done by other scholars of why the situation exists as it exists regarding the problem you research. It is from there where you will develop your new explanations or test the existing one with your data. Readers will take your work seriously if it is based on a particular existing theory.

Third, the literature review shows the way what you propose to study fits in what has already been done about it (the context). You will be able to locate your work in what has been done by just seriously discussing the works of others that are related to your problem of study. Select the ones that highly relate to what you study. They will provide the immediate context of your proposed work.

Fourth, the literature review will show that the problem you propose to investigate is significant and worth researching. Though you spotlighted the significance of the study in the introduction, it will be vivid here when you have reviewed the literature. Readers will clearly note the researches of previous researchers, their contributions, and the actual gap you intend to fill. You have to put a remark of what contributions have the literatures you reviewed contribute and what they do not, which you intend to contribute. You can use statements such as, "So and so's contribution is . . . However, he/she fails to consider his point in the Tanzanian context" (*which you will*

16. Marx quoted in Silverman, *Doing Qualitative Research,* 346.

consider). Or "Despite so and so's contribution, he/she does not address . . ." (*which you will address in your research*).

Fifth, the literature review will show that what you plan to do will produce new *original knowledge*. This is mostly because you will have not found anything that relates to what you want to do in the published literatures that are recent and closely related to your problem of study. In this case, the literature review will show that the knowledge you produce is an *original contribution* to the existing one.

What do we mean by *original knowledge* which you need to contribute in your research work? Let us discuss further this aspect of originality of your contribution to knowledge. Estelle M.Phillips and Derek S. Pugh quoted in Rowena Murray provide us with a more comprehensive definition of it. According to them, in order to make an original contribution you have to do at least one of the following:

> You say something no one has said before.
> You do empirical work that has not been done before.
> You synthesize things that have not been put together before.
> You make a new interpretation of someone else's material/idea.
> You do something in this country that has only been done elsewhere.
> You take an existing technique and apply it to a new area.
> You work across disciplines, using different methodologies.
> You look at topics that people in your discipline have not looked at.
> You test existing knowledge in an original way.
> You add to knowledge in a way that has not been done before.
> You write down a new piece of information for the first time.
> You give a good exposition of someone else's idea.
> You continue an original piece of work.[17]

Therefore by doing at least one of the aspects listed above you will be sure that your research work does something unique; a thing that contributes to what others have done in your field.

The literature review chapter has an introduction, body, and conclusion. In the introduction you promise readers of what they will find in the body of the literature review chapter. It should be done last because it should capture the whole of what has been done. The introduction should tell readers how you structured your review and why structure in that way. Your conclusion of the literature review chapter will summarize the state of scholarship according to your research as you have just reviewed in the

17. Murray, *How to Write*, 70–71.

body of the review. It will also provide a comment about the review and its usefulness in regard to your own work. You explain what your study will do (the thesis statement, the hypothesis you will test, or the research question you will strive to answer), how to do it (the method you will use), and the sources you will use. Through identifying, critically reading and commenting on the literatures, and eventually concluding your review, you will have established your credentials to your readers.

Your literature review must be well–structured following a convincing logical structure for your readers to understand it. The first thing you have to do is to categorize works according to their commonality whether books, journal articles, etc. You will have several groups of works depending on the commonalities they show. The second thing will be to order or arrange them depending on their closeness to your work. The broader theory–based works should be at the top followed by those closer to your work. At the bottom you will have fewer works than at the top of your review (i.e., the funeral-like model of assembling literatures).

In constructing a literature review, select the literatures that are *recent, relevant, and prominent* to your field of study. There is no general rule of the number of literatures to be included in your review. The number of literatures will depend on the convention of the institution to which the report will be submitted. The most important thing is that you have to read the selected literature academically.

What is academic reading of literatures in the literature review process? We speak of academic reading when we consider the nature of secondary literatures. Most secondary literatures are numerous and voluminous. It can take much time reading a very few literatures in whole; and most likely, it can be confusing to the one who does the reading because time cannot be enough to select and read every literature. Unless you focus on what you need, the whole time of your research will be spent on reading very few literatures without even managing to accomplish them.[18]

Therefore, *academic reading* is reading with a *purpose*. Academic reading is not done for just passing time. It focuses on what you want to acquire from a particular literature. Academic reading is goal-oriented. You have to figure out *what* you want to read before you go to the library to search for literatures about it.[19] Epstein, Kenway, and Boden emphasize this point thus:

18. Efron & Ravid, *Action Research*, 21.
19. Efron & Ravid, *Action Research*, 21.

When you read academic work, you need to engage actively with the material by interrogating it. Ask yourself questions as you go along. Do I really agree with this? How convincing is this argument? What holes can I pick in that one? What would I say to the authors if they were explaining their ideas to me in person? How can I make use of these ideas or data to inform my own? What key concept is the author working with and why? If you read actively in this way, your reading will be of positive benefit in keeping up with the development of knowledge in your particular field.[20]

Moreover, academic reading uses skimming and scanning methods to determine whether certain literatures are worth reading in whole, contains spots of what is aimed or does not contain anything important for the problem in question. What you have to do is to understand what you read and extract (write notes) what you need. You do not need to waste time reading the whole work; but you only have to read the places of literatures that speak about what you need while writing fully the documentation aspects of the literature for documentation in the literatures list at the reference section. You need to record what you read because you will have to read many works in different libraries. For sure you will not be able to remember all the works you read, the libraries they are found, and the pages you have read by just depending on the memory of your brain.[21] Therefore it is important to take note of every useful material you find for future use in your work.

Generally speaking, the literature review chapter is more intriguing to actually write it than to just speak about how to write it. A curious reader will rank the importance of this chapter with the importance of the whole research report because the literature review demonstrates your credentials in the context of the credentials of other researchers you have dealt with. It demonstrates your ability to evaluate science and build on it to make your own contribution to it. It will show that you understand your field of study you have engaged in. And therefore, it will show that the work which you have attempted is worth of the reader's attention!

20. Epistein, Kenway & Boden, *Writing for Publication*, 13.
21. Efron & Ravid, *Action Research*, 22.

The Method Chapter

After the readers have believed in the significance of the study based on the literatures review done and the gap of research identified, they will then be interested to know the way (method) which you have used to investigate your problem in order to provide answers to your main research question. Here you have to convince readers that you have selected a good "method" to go about investigating the research problem.[22]

What do we mean by the concept of "method" as we use here in the research report? The concept of method we use here is different from the one we discussed in the chapter on proposal development when distinguishing "method" and "methodology." You can understand the concept of method as used here by conceptualizing the place where one needs to reach. Suppose you want to reach Dar es Salaam city in Tanzania from where you are now. Of course, you cannot just reach there! There must be a means through which you will reach there. This is the *how* part of your aim. Your aim is to reach Dar es Salaam city; but how will you reach there? When we talk of "method" here we mean the way through which to reach your intended destination. You cannot reach Dar es Salaam city (your intended destination) without a justified means to enable you reach there.

In the research report context, the "method" is the whole means through which you investigated the problem to reach to the conclusions you have reached. Here the "method" concept does not only comprise the techniques or tools for data collection as we stated in the proposal development chapter above; it is similar to the methodological perspective in your proposal writing. In this case, some scholars just prefer to call this chapter as a chapter on "methodology" instead of "method." However, our use of the concept of "method" here depicts something even greater than the methodology depicted by these scholars. It depicts something that contains the methodology within it as will be seen in the structure of the method chapter below!

Logically speaking, you cannot pose a problem and reach conclusions about it without doing anything about it towards the conclusions. Those will not be justified conclusions. Justified conclusions need something to be done in order to reach to them. That "something" you do in order to reach to justified conclusions about your research problem is the method, the way, or the means towards the conclusions.

22. Cf.Silverman, *Doing Qualitative Research*, 351—359.

A thoughtful and reliable method strengthens your report because it increases the reliability of the evidence and the conclusions reached. Thoughtful readers will not just accept what you report to them; they will examine the way through which you obtained your evidence and tested your thesis to reach particular conclusions. The method you used must be valid and reliable. It must be genuine and believable to produce reliable research information. Therefore, the method you state in the method chapter stand as a road map to measure the validity and reliability of your conclusions, and possibly of the argument of the whole report.

The structure of the method chapter contains the following components: the introduction, the research design, the methodology, the limitations and delimitations, the ethical considerations and the conclusion. The introduction of the method chapter is a little detailed. It contains the expected achievements, the purpose of the study in brief, and what is discussed in the chapter.

In the research design you address the question: Which paradigm and what type of study do I undertake in order to deal with my research questions? You have to name and discuss the overall paradigm ((positivist, postpositivist or interpretivism) and approach (qualitative, quantitative, or mixed method) you used to investigate the thesis statement and why use that paradigm and approach. You also have to name the design you used as the foundation for your research intervention: is it case study, survey, phenomenological, experiment, content analysis, etc? You have to discuss how does that design work or worked in the context of your research work and what limitations, if any, did it have?

The methodology part will have at least, but not limited to, four important parts: cognitive mode, research instruments, data obtained, and the process of data analysis.

i.   *The Cognitive mode selected*—this part states the cognitive mode you used in gathering information or data from your research, why did you select such cognitive mode, and how it made the research successful or unsuccessful. Is it listening, watching, questioning, reading, or introspection mode?

ii. *Research instruments used*—these are the techniques you used in collecting data in order to analyze and test the thesis statement. Was it interview, questionnaire, or observation? Discuss in detail how did you selected the instrument. What are the advantages and disadvantages of that instrument and how that instrument worked in your proposed research? Discuss how reliable is that instrument and how reliable are the data generated by that instrument. Here you discuss how you obtained your data.

iii. *Data obtained*—After discussing how you obtained your data, here you discuss that data. If your research is qualitative, you discuss the quality of the data you have or expected to have: how did you record the data, was recording correctly done, how did you avoid biasness in you data collection, analysis and discussion of the findings? If you did a quantitative study: the sample you selected, the sampling procedure you used, the population, and how the sample was representative of the larger population (population validity). Discuss the reasons for selecting that particular sample and the sampling procedure you used. Discuss the strengths and weaknesses of the data you obtained, and why do you think the data are still valid for arguing your case despite their weaknesses.

iv. *Data analysis process*—State how you went about analyzing and interpreting the data you had and why use that way of analysis and interpretation. The raw data are useless unless something is done in order to turn them into evidence. "Analysis involves working with data, organizing them, breaking them into manageable units, synthesizing, searching for patterns, discovering what is important and what is to be learned, and deciding what you will tell others. For most projects, the end products of research are dissertations, books, papers, presentations, or (. . .) plans for action."[23] This means that you have to organize, analyze, and interpret them in order to use them as evidence for the argument you present to your readers. Did you do a quantitative analysis? Discuss the statistical techniques you employed and how you interpreted them. Did you do a qualitative analysis? Discuss the way you obtained themes or concepts for interpretation.

In the limitations (methodological weaknesses or flaws) and delimitations (boundaries to which the study deliberately confined itself) part you state what you were able and what you were not able to accomplish using your method. State the limitations (the weak points of your instrument) that will potentially affect the reliability of your data; but tell your readers why the data are still worthwhile despite the limitations stated. State the limitations you faced during research that in one way or another hindered

23. Bogdan & Biklen, *Qualitative Research*, 157.

you from obtaining data and how you dealt with them, e.g., a little number of respondents, the unwillingness of respondents to participate in research, the financial constraints, etc. You also state where your study was confined (delimited) and why confine yourself in that particular part. The delimitation description may be in terms of concepts you confined yourself, study area, and types of definitions you used in your study. Delimitations indicate to the reader the boundaries of your study, areas where you are concerned and not concerned in your study.

In the ethical guidelines part of the method chapter you have to state how you adhered to those guidelines in your work. Name the ethical problems inherent to your research work and how you tackled them following the guidelines: how did you handle issues of anonymity, confidentiality, and informed consent regarding the problems encountered in your research process? How did you minimize harm to you as researcher and to your informants, both physical and psychological? How did you handle issues of plagiarism in your writing stage? All these need a thorough discussion to convince readers that your work followed ethical principles worth of research and report writing.

In the conclusion of the method chapter, provide a brief description of what is presented in the whole chapter and a short outline of the body chapter that follows. This short outline will provide a glimpse of what the reader should expect to see in the body chapters.[24]

The Body Chapters

After the readers are convinced that the method used to investigate the problem was good and appropriate (valid and reliable), they will eventually be interested to see the actual findings of that investigation. They will be interested to see the data presented, the analysis done, and the interpretation of research findings. This is done in terms of several chapters, sub–chapters and sections. Moreover, readers will also be interested in the way you argue for or against, or tests the thesis (hypothesis) statement stated in the introductory chapter.[25]

In writing these chapters, remember the promises you made to your readers before on what will be done. In your introduction, your literature review, and your method chapters you prepared your readers for the real

---

24. Cf. Leedy & Ormrod, *Practical Research*, 324; Moore, *How to do Research*, 133.
25. Cf. Silverman, *Doing Qualitative Research*, 360—372.

cake. The previous chapters provided the smell of that sweet thing ahead of them. In the body chapter, it is the place where you now provide them that long-waited cake to eat. Will they really test the cake they anticipated, a half–cake, or something else? In most cases, it is in this chapter where readers become disappointed because they do not taste the cake promised in the previous chapters; they taste something different. The smell of the promises they have been receiving in the previous chapters does not match with what they are really provided to eat in this chapter. Therefore, this chapter is the heart of your investigation and requires to be taken seriously because it is the one which will determine whether the reader will still be interested to see the conclusions reached or be discouraged altogether.

Components of the Body Chapters

What then are aspects that belong to the body chapters of your research report? In order for the body part of the research report to be convincing as per the previous promises, there are three important things that should be dealt with: presentation of your research findings, your analysis of those findings, and your sub–conclusions about those findings. Thus, this part of the research report is the "findings" part, i.e., the outcomes part of your whole research intervention.

Remember that in the whole of the previous chapters you set a premise on testing or arguing for your thesis. In this part of the research report is where your readers will see that you carefully present your data, analyze, and interpret them in order to argue for or against your thesis. The data you process are the findings for your research. In presenting, analyzing and interpreting them, you are processing them from being "raw data" into "research evidence" that will help you argue or test your thesis (hypothesis) statement.

Remember also that one of the major components of academic (scientific) method involves your ability to make a point through reasoning and evidence. In your research report you need to convince readers that your point of view is correct and worth taking into account. You can do this only if you substantiate your reasons for the point you make with credible evidence. This means that every thesis (hypothesis) or claim you make must be supported by good reasons and tested by facts or evidence. Evidence is the foundation of any academic argument. Hence, any claim made in the chapter, major sections and sub–sections must be strongly supported by credible evidence from your research.

Organizing, Analyzing and Presenting Research Data

We can still ask: Why do you need to organize, present, analyze and interpret research data from your data collection place? As we just pointed out above (in the instruments of data collection chapter), data as raw data are meaningless, useless, and less interesting to other people except to you who collected them and know the way you recorded them. Your readers do not know what they specifically mean. They are not an evidence for them to rely on yet. In order for them to know and understand the meaning of your data, the raw data must be processed. They must be organized in a logical manner, presented in the form of text, chart, tables, photographs, graphs, etc., analyzed and interpreted in order for your readers to understand what they really mean to them. The analysis of the raw data must be done for the purpose of testing the thesis (hypothesis) statement you promised to test in the previous chapters, or developing a new theory (grounded theory) from them. Eventually you should test the thesis (hypothesis) and provide sub–conclusions which will serve in making the main conclusion of the argument of the whole report. The sub–conclusions you make will be found in the sections and sub–sections of the body part. Therefore, the main conclusion of the report at the last chapter is the sum of the sub–conclusions you made in the sections and sub–sections of the report. This means that every sub–conclusion you make in the sections and sub–sections contributes to the main conclusion of the whole report about your thesis statement.

Using Works of other Researchers and Clarity

The body part of your report will also use the works of other researchers. You may want to refute their findings based on yours; you may want to borrow their ideas in order to strengthen yours; you may want to put them forth in order to advance a discussion before you reach a particular sub–conclusion; you may want to use their definitions or ideas in order to enlighten yours, etc. Your readers expect you to "engage" in that game with other scholars in your discussion of findings in order to reach your sub–conclusions. You are really expected to use the works of other scholars to contextualize and support your point of view! In doing this you will need to document, reference, and cite other people's works. We will discuss more about documentation and citation in the forthcoming book called *Writing Well-Organized Course Assignments*.

However, when selecting quotations from your sources, you need to select those that are more convincing ones. Remember, the aim of using other people's materials is not to add to your number of pages; it is to help you argue your case. A convincing quotation speaks directly to the point you want to make. It does not leave readers contemplating and trying to imagine what purpose it serves in that paragraph or sub-section. Therefore, you need to be careful in using other people's materials to the best of your ability.

Avoid pedantic writing which some scholars (to their deaths) use in order to show to their readers that they know their field well. Though pedantic writing makes the report sophisticated, it leaves it less attractive and boring to your readers. It is less attractive and boring because "Pedantic writing uses too many big words, too many abstract ideas and phrases, and too many references to the literature."[26] Remember, the principle is to present the complex ideas you have in the simplest language possible. The use of complex jargons is not acceptable in academic report writing. Mouton affirms: "It is not necessary for a piece of writing to be difficult in order to be properly academic."[27] This means, "Whenever possible use ordinary words, not special technical ones. If you have to use a technical word make sure it is defined the first time you use it."[28] Simple writing will not only make your report fair and attractive to your readers, but also communicative, which is the sole purpose of report writing.

Structuring the Body Chapters

How should you structure the body of your research report? There are no specific ways to use in structuring the body of your research report. This is because different researches investigate different problems, use different methods, do different analyzes and reach different conclusions. The important thing to bear in mind is your creativity in structuring it in the way that readers will understand your argument. However, your report is expected to be divided into chapters of about twenty five pages each. Each chapter

26. Rubin, H.J. & Rubin, I.S., *Qualitative Interviewing*, 268.

27. Mouton, *How to Succeed*, 58.

28. Rubin, H.J & Rubin, I.S., *Qualitative Interviewing*, 268.

represents a major issue of the report. Chapters will be divided into main sections and sub–sections logically divided depending on your preferences. You must always divide your sections and sub–sections logically with a logical order of your argument, avoiding repetitions and making it as simple to understand as possible.

There are several ways to structure your chapters in the body part of the report. The following are some of the possible structures for your data processing chapters:

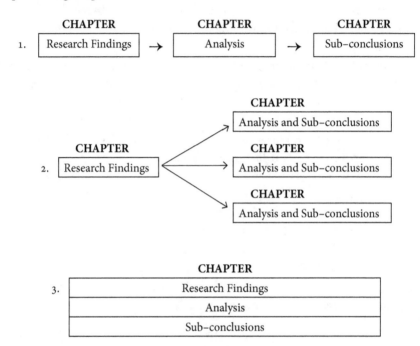

There are also several ways to arrange chapters, sections, and subsections within the report. The possible chapter, section and sub–section division can be as follows:

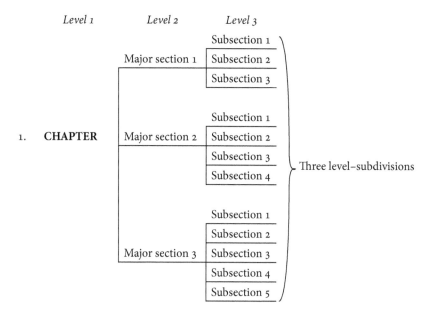

NB: There can be further sub–division to the fourth, fifth, etc., levels. However, we would encourage that reports end with only three levels of sub–sections in order to avoid confusions to readers.

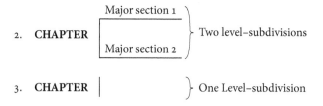

NB: In research reports, it is seldom that a chapter has no sub–divisions. However, if it happens that a chapter does not have, it will be better for readers to understand its content.

Introducing and Concluding the Body Chapters

Be sure to introduce and conclude every chapter in the body part, every major section, and every sub–section. Introductions and conclusions will enable readers to understand where the sub–argument starts and where it ends. They will also be able to relate the sub–argument with what comes before and after it. Introductions and conclusions are powerful tools to lead readers towards understanding your discussion in the body chapters; and hence buying in to you final conclusion of the whole report.

Avoid putting dangling sub–sections because they make no sense for the section. Use linking devices to maintain coherence between chapters, sections, and sub–sections of your report. Some of the devices and their uses are the following: "This implies that . . . " (*for elaborations*), "Stated differently, . . . " (*for reaffirmation*), "Therefore, . . . " (*for making conclusions*), "However, . . . , on the one/other hand . . . " (*for indicating contrasts*), "meanwhile . . . " (*for time*), "furthermore . . . " (*for stating addition*), "on the one/other hand . . ." (*for stating contrasts*), "for example, . . . " (*for showing illustration*), "first . . . second, . . ." (*for listing enumerations*), "in other words . . . " (*for reformulating the statement*), etc. These and many other linking devices will make your ideas linked together and easy for your readers to follow.

Using Evidence obtained from Research to argue Your Case

What are you to do with the evidence you have collected? We said in the beginning of this chapter that the body part of the research report is the "evidence" part. You already have your thesis; you have already collected the data for this thesis, have analyzed and interpreted it turning it into evidence. The major function of evidence is to prove the thesis statement. The thesis statement is your main claim. You need to synthesize the collected data in order to show whether they support or do not support this claim. In order to do that you need to provide substantial reasons to justify your claims and prove them with the evidence you have collected. That is an informed academic argument.

An informed argument is formed through your synthesis of the data collected in order to produce your own new knowledge from that synthesis. In synthesizing the research information, you connect what is in the information you have collected with your own ideas. In this process of synthesizing, you will have to quote the sources of your data directly, summarize or paraphrase the information in the sources while thinking around the information. The synthesis of evidence and your own ideas will be sorely centered upon the thesis or hypothesis of your report, trying to prove or disprove it (for quantitative researches) or the main research question you try to answer (for qualitative researches). This means that the whole of your research report is a synthesis of evidence in connection with your own ideas in order to produce new knowledge.

Proving the thesis (or hypothesis) statement means establishing the validity of it through the evidence you have, to test it as per evidence regarding its quality and usability. You test the thesis (or hypothesis) statement as per its claim. Is the claim valid and hold any water regarding the evidence collected? Does the evidence support it or not? Hofstee asserts: "You should present both evidence that is in favor of your thesis *and* evidence that contradicts it. If you hide evidence that is in opposition to your point of view, you will not arrive at a carefully considered evaluation of your thesis statement."[29] This is proving the thesis statement and is done in every paragraph of the body (evidence) part of the report.

Since every paragraph of every sub-section is a small argument that contributes to the argument of that sub-section, the evidence you have should be incorporated into the relevant paragraphs. In qualitative researches, for example, evidence is presented in the form of excerpts from real verbatim of the source to support a particular theme obtained in the analysis and coding processes. The real words of the source present the world of the source, hence, making the reader to sense the real world of the evidence in the argument of that paragraph.

Hofstee asserts: "The standard sequence is to introduce your argument and the point of it, and then to present and discuss the evidence for it. Then you need to weigh the evidence and arrive at a well-reasoned judgment."[30] The judgment you make is the conclusion of the paragraph. Therefore, the argument of the paragraphs with the evidences in them will make sub-sections, sub-sections will make major sections, major sections will make chapters, and chapters will make the whole research report. Every part mentioned is an argument which serves as a building stone to the argument of the whole report.[31]

The Conclusion Chapter

In the introduction you initiated the research game by providing promises to your readers about what you were going to do. You went on the whole

29. Hofstee, *Constructing a Good Dissertation*, 147.

30. Hofstee, *Constructing a Good Dissertation*, 146.

31. Cf. Leedy & Ormrod, *Practical Research*, 327–329; Moore, *How to do Research*, 133–135.

process doing it. The conclusion chapter tells readers what has been done and its implication. It tells readers what you have discovered in the investigation of your research thesis. This means that it provides the main conclusion to the small conclusions made in the chapters, the sub–chapters and sections. The main thing to bear in mind is that the conclusion chapter concludes about the problem posed in the introduction and the argument to defend the proposed solution (the thesis statement). In that case, what you say in the conclusion should match with what you said in the introduction.

What then should be included in the conclusion chapter of your research report? The following five aspects must be included despite the other aspects you may find necessary: summary of findings, conclusions, summary of contributions to knowledge, recommendations for implementations, and suggestions for further research.[32] Each of these should be presented as a section of its own in order for readers not to be confused. The summary of findings plays a preparatory role. It prepares the reader towards the main conclusions. You have to briefly summarize the sub–conclusions you made in the chapters in order to remind readers before they see the main conclusion. You may also include some materials from the conclusions of some of the sub–sections.

Conclusions are what you can now confidently say about the whole work you have done to deal with your thesis statement, which you actually could not say without the research process you did. Your conclusions may prove or disprove your thesis statement. You need to be honest and faithful to the research work you have done and to the findings you have obtained. In order to be faithful and honest, you need to be open to being challenged by the evidence, or challenging the evidence by using the available evidence. You did not engage in research as a person with a foresight; you engaged in it as a person who was committed to searching for something unknown in order to be known. In that case, whatever comes out is to be accepted. Your conclusions should be fair and justified. You are not supposed to compromise what you are supposed to conclude because readers will question your academic integrity; they will question your ability to do science!

Recommendations for implementation spell out what you would recommend to be done depending on the findings of your research. You have to explain each recommendation giving reasons why that recommendation is important. It may be improvement of a situation, formulation of new policies, etc.

32. Cf. Silverman, *Doing Qualitative Research,* 373 -379.

The summary of contributions presents plainly but concisely what new knowledge has your research added to your field of study depending on the conclusions and findings you have put forth. It should state the theoretical and practical implications of your research work. It should state how it built on the existing knowledge presented in the literature review section, and how it differs from it in terms of new input. Therefore, this section must relate to your literature review chapter, and the significance and objectives in the introductory chapter of the research report.

The suggestion for further research part presents the possible problems to be investigated further. There are more problems than solutions in the world we live in; there are more questions than answers. Your research has provided a solution to just a single problem; however, it has provoked numerous other problems to be sought for solutions. Since scientific research builds on previous researches, it is worthwhile for the research to mention or suggest where specifically should the next researches concentrate in. This will make science live and continuous![33]

Bibliography or Reference List of the Report

You may want to construct a bibliography (the list of all literatures consulted for your work even though not sighted) or a list of references (which includes only the cited works). It will depend very much on the guidelines provided by your university or funding agency. Both of them are advantageous. The bibliography contains a good number of materials about the problem you researched; hence, it becomes a good source for other researchers who will deal with a similar problem in your field. The reference list is short and contains only the cited materials; hence, it makes it easy for readers and examiners to look for something they would prefer to refer to. In whatever the case, bibliography or reference, you need to construct a good list of the works you used for your own work.

Consider how examiners and readers of your work asses the list of materials you used for your work: first, they will examine the number of works you have included in your list. Is it satisfactory according to the topic and type of study undertaken? Readers and examiners will know whether there is extensive or limited number of literatures written about the topic

---

33. Cf. Leedy & Ormrod, *Practical Research*, 329–330; Moore, *How to do Research*, 121–130, 134.

of your study because they are experts or interested people in your field. If your list is too short, it will have a consequence to the quality of your work.

Second, examiners and readers will consider the ratio between books and articles you have used for your work. Some fields have many publications in the form of books and others in the form of articles. The ratio of books to articles will also determine the quality of your report depending on the field of study you are in.

Third, they will consider the types of works you have used mostly. Are there more general works such as textbooks, or those more specialized ones? If your list of works contains more general works than specialized ones, it will bring your readers and examiners into questioning the quality of your work. They will not be satisfied that your work has met the required academic standard, especially in terms of in-depth probing of what was required.

Fourth, they will consider the dates of publication of those materials. Are they recently published or not? If the publications you have listed are old, they will wonder whether you have produced knew knowledge in your research work, especially the ones in the literature review chapter.

Fifth, they will consider the titles of journals and the publishers of books. Are they prestigious or peer–reviewed journals? Are they books published by prestigious and internationally recognized publishers? They will assess the quality of your work depending on the quality of the publishers of books and the quality of journals you have used.

Sixth, they will also consider the authors of books and articles you have used. Are they prominently acknowledged experts on the field? Every field has scholars prominently acknowledged to be experts. If these are not found in your bibliography or list of references, it will obviously reflect your partial survey or use of literatures in your work. You need to make sure that prominent scholars in your field, and in your area of study, have been surveyed and included in your list of works.

All points discussed above, and other related ones, contribute to making the reader identify the quality of secondary literature research you did. A well–researched work will include the relevant contributors in the field, recent publications in recognized peer-reviewed journals, specific contributions from books (not textbooks), and an accepted or convincing number of publications in the list. Therefore, the list of works is also an important part of your research report that needs your utmost attention

Appendices

This part of the report is placed outside the main body just after the list of references or bibliography normally numbered in Roman numbers as a continuation from where the Preliminary Pages ended. It contains some important materials that could not be included in the main body of the report for the sake of space. Their main function is to clarify what is written in the main body. Therefore, they must be referred to somewhere in the main body in order to be placed as appendices. The appendices are named Appendix 1, Appendix 2, etc., or with letters Appendix A, Appendix B, etc., depending on the number of appendices you have.

RE-WRITING YOUR RESEARCH REPORT (EDITING AND REVISING)

The words of Hofstee are important to begin with in this part of report writing: "Knowing something in-depth about your field won't get you a masters or a doctorate degree. Doing a good research won't either. Both are essential, but ultimately you have to write to get a degree. That can be difficult: Some people have a talent for writing, others don't; some have had a lot of practice; others haven't."[34] What Hofstee emphasizes here is that being knowledgeable about the field alone cannot qualify the person to the level of a particular degree. Who knows about the knowledge of the person who purports to know? Doing a good research alone does not also qualify that person to the level of a particular degree either. Who knows about that person's research done? Unless the knowledge is communicated to other people, unless the research done is communicated to other people through writing, you will remain with your good knowledge or your good research unrecognized. Therefore, communicating the findings of research and the knowledge gained is the sole concern of science. Research and knowledge people have about their fields of studies must be disseminated to other people through writings.

34. Hofstee, *Constructing a Good Dissertation*, 193.

Writing to Learn and Writing to Report

However, we would add to the discussion of the previous paragraph that writing and finishing the research report is not enough to qualify your report to a well-written report for a degree. Something else must be done to it. After you have written the first draft of the report, you will have managed to write for your own understanding. This is *"writing to learn."* You understand what you have presented. What follows after the first draft is *"writing to report"* to other people what you have learnt yourself. In order to do that you will have to start the work of rewriting the work for your readers to understand what you learned.[35] Hofstee further reminds us: "A [research report] is not finished when you're done writing. It's finished when you're done editing."[36] Therefore, rewriting is necessary to bring your report to completion. Never be satisfied with the first draft you have just produce, though good looking and neat! You have to rewrite it!

Revising and Editing Your Report

What does it mean by re-writing your research report? Newman enlightens us to the meaning of this core concept in this subsection. According to Neuman, re-writing "involves two processes: revising and editing. *Revising* is inserting new ideas, adding supporting evidence, deleting or changing ideas, moving sentences around to clarify meaning, or strengthening transitions and links between ideas. *Editing* means cleaning up and tightening the more mechanical aspects of writing, such as spelling, grammar, usage, verb tense, sentence length and paragraph organization."[37] Therefore, editing is a component of revising in the process of re-writing your report. In re-writing your report you need to ask yourself at least three questions: first, how well does this report answer the question I stated in the introduction chapter? Second, have I forgotten any point that could strengthen the argument of my report? And third, is my report well-structured and ideas in it linked together to provide a coherent argument?

---

35. Cf. Punch & Qancea, *Introduction to Research*, 369.

36. Hofstee, *Constructing a God Dissertation*, 199.

37. Numan, *Social Research*, 470.

The Process of Rewriting

In answering the questions above, what then should you be editing and revising for in the process of rewriting for your readers' understanding? Several aspects need your attention in the editing and revising process according to Neuman[38]: first, edit and revise for the better structure of your report. Every point regarding the structure should be checked and ensured to be where it is supposed to be. All repetitions and misplacements must be rectified. Every heading or sub–heading must be checked and edited where possible. Shorter headings are better than longer ones. Check the matches between the points you make and the respective sections or sub–section. Rectify any irrelevant points you notice.

Second, edit and revise for the better flow of your argument. Make sure that it is convincing. This means that you have to double–check it to see that it is *logical*. Check the linking devices that they are placed where they are supposed to be. Check that there is a natural flow (coherence) of the argument for your readers to understand it. In editing and revising the flow do three important things: check how to the point your argument is; how ideas which make up an argument link together; and which structure of the argument you have selected for a particular paragraph. The structure of the argument has to be straightforward for readers to follow. Moreover, make sure that the introduction and conclusion of every part are effective and convincing.

Third, edit and revise for clarity and concreteness of evidence you placed in the paragraphs and appendices. Double–check to be sure that the evidence that supports your argument is *credible*. Make sure that there is no claim that is left unsupported by evidence. You have to edit for evidence thoroughly. This means that you have to read and re-read and re-read your work during the editing stage, not for your own understanding but for your readers' understanding. Make sure that the evidence you placed is credible and what it is intended to support. Any weak evidence must be improved or replaced by a stronger one available.

Fourth, edit and revise for *accuracy* of mathematical or statistical information. Check the calculations and statistical information to be sure that they are correct. Bear in mind that small mistakes in the calculations or statistical information may mislead the reader towards understanding the argument. They need to be checked meticulously for accuracy.

38. Neuman, *Social Research*, 471.

Fifth, edit and revise for *precision* of grammatical aspects (word orders, agreement of subjects and verbs used, nouns used, correctness of articles, the relative pronouns who, which, and that and the relative clauses accompanying them, and the use of correct tenses) and diction (the proper choice and use of words). Precision has to do with saying exactly what you mean by selecting the right words and the right level of depth in explaining a certain matter. You have to check the grammar of sentences, their accuracy, tenses, punctuations, spelling errors and spelling consistence (British or American), accuracy in capitalization, clarity of sentences and phrases, and sentence length to suit your intention. These aspects, if not checked, may be obstacles to the reader towards understanding the presented argument. Moreover, avoid any informal diction in your writing: avoid colloquialism (language of everyday communication or spoken language), slang (language known to a particular group of people), regionalism (language known within a particular geographical location), or non–standard diction (words not included in Standard English). Therefore, edit and revise to be sure that you always use formal diction in your entire report.

Sixth, edit and revise for *consistency* of formatting style to suit your institution's style. Check that the guidelines of you institution are thoroughly adhered to. Rectify any places that do not match the guidelines. The guidelines should be followed to the letter because they are the ones that will make your report academically acceptable in that institution.

Seventh, edit and revise for *appropriateness* of the voice used in the report. You have to balance the way you use active and passive voices in your report. Most researchers prefer using passive voice to active. Academic writing sounds well and stimulates the reader if active voice is used because the sentences clearly show the actor of the action. In the passive voice the actor is hidden and this leaves readers with a question of who did the action purported by the sentence. Thus, as Toby Fulwiler asserts: "Passive constructions are indirect, tiresome, and risk putting readers to sleep."[39]

However, the principle of using active voice rather than passive needs further attention. Though the active voice shows clearly the subject who does the action, it still does not show the intention and main focus of the author. In scientific writing, and for the sake of precision, the intention of the author is important. In this case, you will have to use passive voice in some sentences depending on your purpose and focus. In order to clarify this point, consider the following sentences:

39. Fulwiler, *College Writing*, 182.

1. *Students are considered* stupid if they do not accomplish their course works.

2. *We consider* students stupid if they do not accomplish their course works.

In the first sentence above, the main focus of the author is on "students" and their malingering habits. The author is not interested in the anonymous person who considers the habit of students. In this case, the passive voice becomes a correct option. In the second sentence, the main focus is the "We," the subject who considers the habit of students. If the intention of the author is to show who considers the habit of students, then the second sentence becomes the correct option.

In addition, active and passive voices depend very much on the kind of action. Consider the following sentences:

1. *It is suggested* that people should drink clean and safe water.

2. Health officers suggest that people should drink clean and safe water.

Here, the second sentence is more appropriate because the anonymous "It" does not link the reader to the actor of the action. It still leaves a question because "It" is undefined and ambiguous to understand. The active voice is appropriate to use when referring to the action which a person performs. Actions such as suggest, argue, claim, indicate, promise, show, etc., preferably go with active voice. However, the principle will still remain: the intention and focus of the author

Eighth, edit and revise to ensure that you are consistent in the use of the person. *Consistency* matters greatly in your report writing in any aspect that repeats itself within the report. Are you using first or third person in your report? Some scholars (to their own deaths) recommend using the third person (he, she, it, or the researcher) in the research report. This is the great emphasis for most quantitative researchers. According to them, using the third person makes the report more objective and the author of the report becomes more neutral. Their measuring instruments, e.g., questionnaires, are not interactive either. They make them distanced from their informants through avoiding to mention the first names of people and the use of passive voices.[40]

In fact, we would recommend using the first person in both researches, especially in qualitative researches where the measuring instruments,

40. Bogdan & Biklen, *Qualitative Research in Education*, 190–191.

e.g., observations and interviews, are greatly interactive. You as qualitative researcher are not distanced from your research informants. The use of first person makes the report live; you become more visible, honest, subjective, and easily identified with the written report. When you use the "third person" pronouns and the words like "the researcher," avoid first names in your reporting and use some passives to hide the actor, you bring to your report the connotation of objectivity that hardly exists in reality. You are trying to distance yourself from the report which has just been written by yourself. Qualitative research report writers mention the first names of people, and mostly use active voices where appropriate. However, whatever the person or style of writing you select to use, you have to be consistent throughout the research report.[41]

Ninth, edit for removing any hate or offensive language. Check to ensure that you rectify any sexist, stereotyping (judgmental, denigrating, defaming or demeaning language in terms of age, class, racial or ethnic group), or language with any kind of biasness in whatever terms. Consider the following gendered words and their possible non–gendered alternatives in parentheses: policeman (*police officer*), poetess (*poet*), chairman (*chairperson*), landlord (*land owner*); manmade (*synthetic*), postman (*post agent*), maid (*domestic*), air hostess (*flight attendant*), etc. Research does not aim at intimidating or denigrating readers in terms of gender, age, or group they belong. Rather, it aims at making them comfortable with the results obtained. The language you use to address various groups of people will determine the fulfillment of this research aim. Check the personal pronouns you use and the way you address the various races or categories of people.[42]

Tenth edit and revise the research report manuscript for correctness of minor issues. This is proofreading. Proofreading involves reading again the manuscript after it is finished in order to check for typing (*typos*) mistakes and correcting them. Proofread for the correctness of spellings, punctuations, paragraph arrangements, and rhythms of phrases and sentences. Where possible read the whole paragraph aloud to sense the way you hear the words, phrases, and sentences in it.[43]

In order to be consistent and not keep on editing and revising, edit and revise sequentially from the largest part of your work to the smallest units. In summary, begin with the overall structure of your work to

41. Ibid.

42. Fulwiler, *College Writing*, 183.

43. Ibid.

make sure that it is in order. Edit and revise the internal structure of the small units that comprise the report (sections, sub–sections and chapters) to ensure that they are in order. After editing the structure edit the flow of your argument and the way you used the evidence. Then edit and revise the various formulas, graphs, mathematical or statistical materials you used. Then edit and revise the sentences and paragraphs. Eventually check and edit the formalities as per your institution. In the editing and revising stage, you need to be as meticulous as possible. Make sure that you read your work for perfection.

WHY DO MOST RESEARCH REPORTS FAIL?

In the above-paragraphs we discussed the ways in which you can make your research report convincing, attractive, and acceptable to your funding agency or for your course requirement in your department. There are also several aspects that can make your research report unacceptable. According to Dawson, the report can be failed or rejected if:

1. There is no logical structure.
2. Ideas are not well thought out.
3. [The] Work is disorganised.
4. Assumptions are made which cannot be justified by evidence.
5. There are too many grammatical and spelling mistakes.
6. Sentences and/or paragraphs are too long or too obscure.
7. It is obvious that ideas and sentences have been taken from other sources.
8. There is too much repetition.
9. There is too much irrelevant information.
10. Summary and conclusions are weak.[44]

Therefore, your attention to the aspects listed above is required in the process of re–writing your report in order to ensure its acceptability.

44. Dawson, *Introduction to Research*, 143.

CONCLUSION

This chapter focused on writing a good scientific research report from the beginning to the end. We have argued in this chapter that writing the first draft makes you understand what you argue in the report. However, your aim is to communicate what you understand to your intended audience. In order to communicate the findings to your audience, you have to re-write the report. You have to painfully and meticulously edit and revise the components of the research report for readers to understand the presented argument. Editing and revising needs care and meticulousness to large and minor issues that can obscure the intended meaning of the presented arguments.

After you have struggled to edit and re–edit and revise your research report provide it to someone else to read for remaining errors that can hinder your readers to understand your argument. Ask him or her to check for the consistence in structure, argument, evidence, and conclusions. Remember that this person is not supposed to write sections chapters or anything new for you. This person has to deal with what you have presented in your report to make it as perfect and as professional as possible.[45] A good and well–edited and revised research report is consistent in structure and in the way it presents the argument; it is easy to read, and is professional.

In whatever the case, "Don't expect satisfaction in your writing to come from other people. You'll be sorely disappointed. Satisfaction in your writing has to come from within. It is the realization that you have done a good work."[46] Having finished all the stages of report writing discussed in this chapter, and at last satisfied with what you have done, elegantly submit the research report where it is required for evaluation!

FURTHER READING LIST

Leedy & Ormrod, *Practical Research*, 323–348.
Moore, Nick, *How to do Research*, Second Edition, 121–145.
Silverman, *Doing Qualitative Research*, 2013:333–381.

45. Neuman, *Social Research*, 470.

46. Alley, *The Craft of Scientific Writing*, 253.

Chapter 7

RULES OF THE ACADEMIC GAME

"The scientific community is governed by a set of professional norms and values that researchers learn and internalize during many year of schooling. The norms are mutually reinforcing and contribute to the unique role of the scientist. (. . .) Scientists [in a particular field] largely check on each other to see that the norms are followed."

—**Neuman,** *Social Research,* **9**

INTRODUCTION

THE ACADEMIC (OR SCIENTIFIC) GAME is similar to any other games we know. It is similar to football, handball, cricket, volleyball, etc. As we know, every game has its rules to follow in order to maintain order and harmony when implementing the game. Every player has to adhere to the rules of that particular game in order for him or her to be a member among other players. If the player violets the prescribed rules of that game, that player has to be punished. Punishments vary for each game: from payment, suspension from participating in certain matches to expulsion from the term as a whole. Therefore, rules make harmony and order possible among players, among coaches, and in the relationship between coaches and players.

Players in a particular game do not become players of that game automatically, and neither do coaches. They become players or coaches after undergoing a certain training and initiation. They are trained by senior players who are experienced players of the game. Senior players are the ones who eventually initiate them after verifying that they have adhered to the prescribed rules of the game. Senior players initiate them after being satisfied with their level of training received and after demonstrating that they are qualified for that game. It means that junior players prove to the senior players that they are capable of following the prescribed rules of the game in order for them to be initiated into being either full coachers or players.

THE ACADEMIC OR SCIENTIFIC GAME

The word "science" comes from Latin "*scientia*," which means "knowledge." This means that science is a systematic search for knowledge about existing phenomena that are unknown to us through the application of the scientific method. Science goes beyond the taken–for–granted knowledge; it goes beyond what people commonly assume as being the true, or the normal. Therefore, the academic or scientific game as a systematic search for knowledge is not exempted from having rules or norms. The academic game is a game with sophisticated rules to follow. Players of the academic game explore the world around them in order to deal with tangible problems of human life. Players of the academic game do not evolve automatically; they are trained and initiated in different levels. This means that they internalize them as they practice science in their schooling.[1]

The main aim of all academic ranks from certificates, diplomas, bachelors, masters, and doctorates is to measure how people follow academic rules pertaining to the level they aspire in a particular field of study. Senior academicians measure them and determine whether to initiate or refuse to initiate them in the academic rank aspired for. Therefore, being an academic is not just boasting that you are because you know many things around you. It involves proving to other academics in your level and field of study about the way you are capable of following the rules of the academic game in order to foster your academic integrity.

1. Cf. Neuman, *Social Research*, 9.

RULES IN THE ACADEMIC GAME

Which are the rules of the academic game that one has to follow in order to be a good player of this game? This chapter concludes the book by reminding you the rules of this scientific or academic game. There are many rules and sub–rules students have to follow depending on the type of field they are in, the academic level they aspire, and the institution they belongs to. However, the major ones concern the following important aspects: the obligation to produce an original academic work (your own work), to follow ethical obligations in producing that work, valuing works of other academics (not falsifying them irresponsibly), and avoiding plagiarism at all costs. The following are some of the individual rules of the academic game.[2]

First, in your research and construction of an academic work you can approach and discuss your ideas and seek advice from anybody. But you are not allowed to let those people construct a research problem, shape it, do the literature review, write the method and eventually write the research report for you. You are the one who has to do the work honestly not them. This means that the research work you produce must be originally yours reflecting your own integrity.

Second, in your search for secondary materials to support your research done, you are free to use librarians to find them because they know where they are found. However, you are not allowed to let them read for you and provide you the notes of the relevant parts of your research problem. You are the one to do the reading of the materials and construct notes according to your intellect and point of view. You have to produce your own original work that does not depend on the librarians.

Third, you are allowed to borrow methods of other researchers; you can also seek advice from them on how to apply these methods to your work. However, you are not allowed to let them write that method or apply it in your work for you. You are the one to write up the method according to the advice you have received and apply it to your work according to your own creativity and ability. Though you have borrowed the method, it is you who has to do the research following the method you just borrowed. The work done must be originally yours, not theirs.

Fourth, in order to obtain more ideas, or refresh your own ideas, you can chat or discuss your ideas, or your argument, interpretation and conclusions with other people. You can also seek for comments or suggestions

2. Cf. Mligo, *Doing Effective Fieldwork*, 32–33.

from others about your work. However, you are not allowed to let them argue, analyze, interpret or conclude the work for you. You are the one who has to do all these tasks. You can consider their comments and suggestions and use them in your work in your own way. The produced work must be originally yours, not of the people you consulted for advice, comments, and suggestions.

Fifth, in nourishing your work towards a consistent, readable and professional academic work, you can use a professional editor for that task. However, you are not allowed to let the professional editor interfere with your problem of research, thesis, method, presentation, analysis of data and the way you have decided to communicate your findings. The editor's main concern is rectifying the technical issues that hinder your work from being consistent, easy to read and professional, e.g., grammar, flow of materials, use of transitional phrases, omissions, repetitions, and redundancies. The work should reflect your own ability to think, do research, and communicate it to your readers. It should not, in any away, reflect the ability of the editor. You have to present to your editor the guidelines of your institution so that that editor follows them during the editing process. Moreover, you need to check and re-check again the edited work to ensure that the editing done by your editor was according to your preferences.

Sixth, follow all ethical guidelines prescribed by your institution to the letter. Guidelines ensure that the academic work does not cause anyone among participants in your research to be harmed during the collection of data, or during the dissemination of the final results. Always remember that participants are vulnerable to harm, especially if the data they provide are sensitive. The ethical guidelines followed should be stipulated clearly in the method chapter.[3]

Seventh, be open in the whole of your research, especially to your participants. Academic work is built on openness and trust. You have to be open to your fellow academics (scientists) about the idea you have, the problem you research, the method you use, the type of literatures you intend to use, and whatever necessary for them to know. They can provide you important suggestions to advance your academic work.

Neuman emphasizes about the above-mentioned rule when he writes: "Scientific knowledge must be shared with others; it belongs to everyone. Creating scientific knowledge is a public act, and the findings are public property, available for all to use. (. . .) New knowledge is not formally

3. Mouton, *How to Succeed*, 238–245.

accepted until other researchers have reviewed it and it has been made publicly available in a special form and style."[4] Therefore, openness to other people about one's research and the research findings is the prerequisite of any researcher.

However, in doing that you need to be careful that the issues of confidentiality and anonymity regarding your informants are strictly adhered to. You share openly what you think requires sharing. Make sure that you are open to criticisms and oppositions. Take any criticism and opposite idea positively. Criticisms and opposite ideas should be catalysts to you to think further about your own work. Force no participants to participate in your research work. Let them be free to participate or not participate. Be open to them about what is required of them as they participate and leave them to decide for themselves or not. This means that you have to obtain an informed consent from research participants before conducting research to them.

Eighth, you should avoid any kind of fraud in research. Fraud in research includes, but not limited to, the following behaviors:

a) *Fabrication of data*—You should not temper to "cook" data or alter the data you obtained from your research to suit your thesis or research problem. This is called fabrication or falsification of data. Remember your research was not done to prove your research thesis right! It was done in order to uncover the reality from the area of research in order to *test* your thesis. Testing your thesis involves proving it right or wrong, testing it whether it is supported by the collected data or not. The more supported it is, the more it comes near to the truth. Anything is expected and you should accept whatever reality which the data will present. You need to remain a faithful servant of science in whatever circumstances! If you do not believe in what the data assert, you are free to argue against them when discussing them. However, you have to present, analyze them, and interpret them as they are. Tempering to cook data or alter the obtained data in any way in order for them to look better is against the practice of science.[5]

b) *Selecting only the best data to be published.* A good researcher is the one who handles research information as were obtained from the research process. There are no better or worse data. When it comes

---

4. Neuman, *Social Research*, 9.

5. Leedy and Ormrod, *Practical Research*, 229; Ary, Jacobs, Sorensen & Walker, *Introduction to Research*, 102–103.

to using them as evidence to support an argument you need to select the ones that provide stronger (not best) support to what you try to convey in order to publish them. This means that the selection of data should base on the strength they have to support your argument, not on how better they look in your sight.

c) *Publishing stolen or plagiarized work.* Publishing a stolen or plagiarized work is cheating your readers. It is making them believe that what you convey to them belongs to you. Plagiarism is one of the fatal academic offences severely punished. One way to avoid publishing stolen works is to avoid plagiarism in all costs.

d) *Claiming as your credit for a work done by someone else.* For example, if a student proposes a research idea, reviews the literatures, formulates a research problem, research questions, designs the research, executes the research and writes the report after analyzing and interpreting the data, then the professor takes a senior status in the publication of that research; that is a typical fraud.

e) *Appending your name to a work that you have little to do with it.* Though you may have a minor input in that work, that input does not warrant your authorship of that work. For example, the lecturer may provide a group assignment to three students to work together. However, only one student concentrates in the work, and the other two contribute some few sentences each and attach their names as full authors of the work. That is a typical fraud.

The words of Neuman are important here to emphasize on the above-discussed scientific rule when he writes: "Scientists must be neutral, impartial, receptive, and open to unexpected observations or new ideas. They should not be rigidly wedded to a particular idea or point of view. They should accept, even look for, evidence that runs against their positions and should honestly accept all findings based on high–quality research."[6]

Ninth, keep the raw data you obtained from research and the references of the sources where you obtained them at a safe place. For the sake of anonymity, nobody is allowed to have access to these raw data except you who collected them. Your readers will be accessed to the processed (organized, presented, analyzed and interpreted) data, not the raw data and the references of their sources. Therefore, for the sake of confidentiality and anonymity raw data should be kept at a place where nobody can have

---

6. Neuman, *Social Research*, 9.

access. These data are for your future references and for whatever happens that can lead you to referring to them; or for future analysis to serve a different purpose, e.g., further dissemination of research in the form of articles and papers.[7]

Tenth, do not plagiarize other people's works. Plagiarism, as a kind of fraud, is using other people's words or ideas either calling them yours or implying that they are yours. This means that you use other people's works without acknowledging the sources where you have consulted. You must be honest to acknowledge other people's works whenever you use them. This means that you have to use other people's works responsibly; you have to provide a reference for every source of the idea or words you borrow from others. In doing that, your work will be credible and academically valuable when your readers see it.[8] Neuman emphasizes: "Scientists demand honesty in all research; dishonesty or cheating in scientific research is a major taboo."[9] Hence, as Deane Pecorari advises: "To avoid plagiarism and to be safe from accusations of it, students need to know how to use sources in a way which is not only acceptable to *some* readers but also unlikely to attract criticism from *any* reader."[10]

CONCLUSION

The rules discussed above form part of the scientist's or researcher's commitment to the search for truth about the world around us. It involves a contract not written on paper but intrinsic in your conscience. Mouton calls this commitment or contract as your "epistemic imperative."[11] By "epistemic imperative" Mouton implies that the contract that you enter to the search for truth is not negotiable; it is intrinsic and imperative to every scientific inquiry conducted. In this case, membership to the team of academics, scientists, or researchers involves a commitment to the search for truth. This search for truth concerns a commitment to following the

7. Cf. Fraenkel, Warren & Hyun, *How to Design and Evaluate*, 63–64, Mouton, *How to Succeed*, 243–244.

8. Saldanha & O'Brien, *Research Methodologies*, 48–49; Mligo, *Writing Academic Papers*, 63–87; Neuman, *Social Research Methods*, 9.

9. Neuman, *Social Research Methods*, 9.

10. Pecorari, *Academic Writing*, 40 (emphasis is in original).

11. Mouton, *How to Succeed*, 239.

prescribed rules of the scientific game which members of the scientific community largely check on each other to see that they are duly followed.[12]

FURTHER READING LIST

Saldanha & O'Brien. *Research Methodologies in Translation Studies* (2013).
Leedy & Ormrod. *Practical Research* (2014).
Neuman, *Social Research Methods*, 2000:9–10.

12. Cf. Neuman, *Social Research Methods*, 9.

Appendix A

COMMONLY USED ABBREVIATIONS
IN RESEARCH REPORT WRITING

App.	Appendix
chap.	Chapter
ed.	Edition
1st ed.	First Edition
2nd ed.	Second Edition
3rd ed.	Third Edition
4th ed.	Fourth Edition
Ed. (Eds.)	Editor (Editors)
No.	Number (as in No.1, No.2, No.3, etc)
Nos.	Numbers (as in Nos. 1, 2, 3, . . .)
p. (pp.)	page (pages)
Rev. ed.	Revised Edition
Supp.	Supplement
Trans.	Translator
Vol.	Volume (as in Volume 1, Volume, 2, Volume 3, etc)
vols.	volumes (as in two volumes, three volumes, etc)

LATIN EXPRESSIONS IN RESEARCH REPORT WRITING

SHORT EXPRESSIONS REFERRING TO TEXTUAL MATTERS

Expression	Its Full Form	Its Literal Meaning	Its Modern Academic Use
cf.	*Confer*	Compare	Compare
e.g.	*exempli gratia*	free example	for example
et. al.	*et alii*	and others	and other authors
etc.	*et cetera*	and other things	and others
erratum	*erratum*	an error	a typographical error/mistake
errata	*errata*	errors	a list of typographical errors /mistakes
ibid.	*ibidem*	in the same place	the same reference as the previous
i.e.	*id est*	that is	that is to say
infra	*infra*	below	see below
loc. cit.	*loco citato*	in the place cited	in the place cited
N.B	*nota bene*	note well	take note
op.ct.	*opere citato*	in the work cited	in the work cited
passim	*passim*	here and there	the point is made in several places
P.S.	*Post scriptum*	after writing	something added after the signature
sic	*sic*	thus	the error in the original quote
supra	*supra*	above	see above
viz.	*videlicent*	obviously	namely
vs.	*versus*	against	against

LATIN TEXTUAL EXPRESSIONS STARTING
WITH A PREPOSITION

a fortiori—with even stronger reason, by a more convincing argument

a posteriori—reasoning based on past experience, reasoning from effect to cause

a priori—reasoning that precedes experience, reasoning from cause to effect.

ab initio—from the beginning

ad hoc—for a specific occasion, not based on regular operations, informal (e.g., an ad hoc meeting, solution to the problem, etc.)

ad infinitum—to infinity, it is so without limit, forever.

ad lib—done at will

ante meridium—before noon (abbreviated a.m, or A.M)

antebellum—before the war, usually before the American Civil War

circa (c. or ca.)—about, approximately, usually used with dates or numbers

de facto—from the fact, it existing by fact not by right (e.g., the de facto king)

de jure—from the law, it exists by right (the de jure leadership)

ex post facto—after the fact, it is so retrospectively

in memorium—in a memory of a person

in situ—in its original or appointed place (e.g., the research conducted *in situ*)

in toto—in whole, or in its entirety

in vitro—in a glass (e.g., most biological experiments are conducted *in vitro*)

in vivo—in life, experiments conducted on living organisms

inter alia—among other things

ipso facto—in that very fact

per capita—per head (e.g., the Tanzanian *per capita* income is 10,000/-)

per diem—per day, expenses allowed each day (e.g., his *per diem* is 80,000/-)

post factum—after something has happened

post meridiem—after noon (abbreviated p. m, or P.M, e.g., we meet at 1.30 p.m) *postmoterm*—after death, an examination to determine the cause of death

pro rata—in proportion (e.g., *pro rata* payments for part time working)

sine die—without a day, with no time fixed for the next meeting

sine qua non—without which not, hence an essential precondition for something

OTHER COMMON LATIN EXPRESSIONS IN ACADEMIC REPORT WRITING

Anno Domin (A.D)—in the year of the Lord, the number of year after the beginning of Christianity (e.g., He was born in A.D 1969)

bona fide—in good faith, genuine, sincere (e.g., he is a *bona fide* student of this school, or he had a *bona fide* effort to help solve the problem)

coveat—a caution or warning (e.g., *coveat* emptor, "Let the buyer beware")

ceteris peribus—other things being equal (used by economists)

Curriculum Vitae (CV)—summary of one's educational and academic achievements

ego—I, being conscious of or projecting to oneself, individual's perception of oneself (e.g., In order to satisfy his own *ego*, he decided to probe what was underneath)

locus classicus—the standard or most authoritative source of an idea or reference

quid pro quo—something for something, to provide or ask for something in return for a favor or service

status quo—things as they are, the normal or standard situation (e.g., one of the aims of research is to challenge the *status quo*)

sui generis—unique

viva vorce—an oral examination (e.g., You will have to appear for a *viva vorce* two months after completing and submitting your PhD Dissertation)

Appendix C

LIST OF SOME KEY VERBS USED
FOR STATING RESEARCH OBJECTIVES

Analyze	Devise	Highlight	Prescribe	Solve
Appraise	Diagnose	Identify	Prioritize	Sort
Assess	Differentiate	Illuminate	Probe	Specify
Calculate	Discern	Illustrate	Process	Standardize
Categorize	Discover	Implement	Produce	Streamline
Clarify	Distinguish	Improve	Progress	Study
Classify	Establish	Indicate	Prove	Synthesize
Collate	Estimate	Integrate	Quantify	Tabulate
Compare	Evaluate	Invent	Query	Test
Contrast	Examine	Investigate	Recommend	Trace
Construct	Execute	Itemize	Reconstruct	Transform
Create	Expand	Judge	Refine	Translate
Demonstrate	Experiment	List	Reform	Underline
Derive	Explain	Locate	Reveal	Understand
Detect	Explore	Measure	Review	Unite
Describe	Fix	Modify	Scrutinize	Use
Design	Formulate	Organize	Show	Validate
Develop	Generate	Outline	Simplify	Verify

References

Alley, Michael. *The Craft of Scientific Writing*. New York, New York: Springer Science+Business Media, 1996.

Ary, Jacobs, Sorensen & Walker, *Introduction to Research in Education*, Ninth Edition. Belmont, California: Wadsworth, 2014.

Axelrod, Bradley N, & James Windell. *Dissertations Solutions: A Concise Guide to Planning, Implementing and Surviving the Dissertation Process*. Lanham, Maryland: Rowman and Littlefield Education, 2012.

Andrews, Molly, Corinne Squire and Maria Tamboukou (eds.). *Doing Narrative Research*. Los Angeles: Sage, 2008.

Angrosino, Michael. *Doing Ethnographical and Observational Research*. Los Angeles: Sage, 2007.

Barbour, Rosaline. *Interpreting Qualitative Research: A Student's Guide*. Los Angeles: Sage, 2014.

Bogdan, Robert C. & Biklen, Sari Knopp. *Qualitative research in Education: An Introduction to the Theory and Method*. Needham Heights, Massachussetts.: Allyn & Bacon, 1998.

Booth, Wayne C., Gregory G. Colomb and Joseph M. Williams. *The Craft of Research*. Chicago and London: The University of Chicago Press, 2003.

Casley, D.J. and D.A. Lury. *Data Collection in Developing Countries*. Second Edition. Oxford: Clarendon, 1987.

Cresswell, J.W. *Educational Research: Planning, Conducting, and Evaluating Quantitative and Qualitative Research*. Fourth Edition. Boston, Massachussetts., Pearson, 2012.

Conrad, Clifton F. and Ronald C. Serlin. *The SAGE Handbook for Research in Education: Engaging Idea and Enriching Inquiry*. Thousand Oaks, California: Sage, 2006.

Corbetta, Piergiorgio. *Social Research: Theory, Methods and Techniques*. Thousand Oaks, California.: Sage, 2003.

Dawson, Catherine. *Introduction to Research: A Practical Guide for Anyone undertaking a Research Project*. Fourth Edition. Oxford: How to Content, 2009.

Efron, Sara Efrat and Ruth Ravid, *Action Research in Education: A Practical Guide*. New York, New York: The Guilford Press, 2013.

Epstein, Debbie, Jane Kenway, and Rebecca Boden. *Writing for Publication*. London: Sage, 2005.

Field, Andy and Graham Hole. *How to Design and Report Experiments*. London: Sage, 2003.

Fink, Arlene, & Jacqueline Kosecoff, *How to Conduct Surveys: A Step-by-Step Guide.* Beverly Hills, California: Sage, 1985.

Foster, Peter. "Observational Research." In *Data Collection and Analysis*, edited by Sapsford, Roger and Victor Jupp, 57–92. Second Edition. London: Sage, 2006.

Fraenkel, Warren & Hyun, *How to Design and Evaluate Research in Education.* Eighth Edition. New York, New York: McGraw-Hill, 2012.

Fulwiler, Toby. *College Writing: A Personal Approach to Academic Writing.* Third Edition. Portsmouth, NH.: Boynton/Cook, 2002.

Gerber, Alan S. and Donald P. Green. *Field Experiments: Design, Analysis and Interpretation.* New York, New York.: W.W. Norton and Company, 2012.

Gillham, Bill. *Developing a Questionnaire.* Second Edition. London: Continuum, 2007.

Gobo, Giampietro. *Doing Ethnography.* London: Sage, 2008.

Glaser, Barney and Anselm Strauss. *The Discovery of Grounded Theory: Strategies for Qualitative Research.* New York, New York.: Aldine de Gruyter, 1999.

Glaser, Barney. *Theoretical Sensitivity: Advances in the Methodology of Grounded Theory.* Mill Valley, California.: Sociology Press, 1978.

Gorden, Raymond. *Basic Interviewing Skills.* Itasca, IL: F.E. Peacock, 1992.

Hancock, Dawson R. & Bob Algozzine. *Doing Case Study Research: A Practical Guide for beginning Researchers.* Second Edition. New York, New York: Teachers College Press, 2011.

Harvey, Lee. *Critical Social Research.* London: Unwin Hyman, 1990.

Hofstee, Erik. *Constructing a Good Dissertation: A Practical Guide to Finishing a Master's, MBA or PhD on Schedule.* Sandton, South Africa: Exactica, 2006.

Johnson, Burke. & Christensen, Larry. *Educational research: Quantitative and Qualitative Approaches.* Needham Heights, Massachussetts: Allyn & Bacon, 2000.

Kothari, C.R. *Research Methodology: Methods and Techniques.* New Delhi: New Age International, 2004.

Koul, Lokesh. *Methodology of Educational Research.* Third Revised Edition. New Delhi: Vikas, 1984.

Kumar, *Research Methodology: A Step-by-Step Guide for Beginners.* London: Sage, 2005.

Leedy, Paul D. and Jeanne Ellis Ormrod. *Practical Research: Planning and Design.* Essex: Pearson, 2014.

Machi, Lawrence A. and Brenda T. McEvoy. *The Literature Review.* Thousand Oaks, California: Corwin, 2009.

Mann, Peter H. *Methods of Social Investigation.* Second Edition. Oxford: Basil Blackwell, 1985.

McDonald, Roderick P. *Test Theory: A Unified Treatment.* Mahwah, New Jersey: Lawrence Erlbaum Associates, 1999.

Mligo, Elia .Shabani. *Jifunze Utafiti: Mwongozo kuhusu Utafiti na Uandishi wa Ripoti yenye Mantiki.* Dar es Salaam: Ecumenical Gathering, 2012a.

_____. *Writing Academic Papers: A Resource Manual for Beginners in Higher-Learning Institutions and Colleges.* Eugene, Oregon.: Wipf and Stock/Resource, 2012.

_____. *Doing effective Fieldwork: A Textbook for Students of Qualitative Field Research in Higher-Learning Institutions.* Eugene, Oregon: Wipf and Stock/Resource, 2013.

Moore, Nick. *How to do Research.* Second Edition. London: The Library Association, 1987.

Mouton, Johann. *How to succeed in Your Master's and Doctoral Studies: A South African Guide and Resource Book.* Pretoria: Van Schaik, 2001.

Murray, Rowena. *How to Write a Thesis.* Third Edition. Meidenhead: McGraw Hill, Open University Press, 2011.

Myrdal, Gunnar. *Objectivity in Social Research.* Middletown: Wesleyan University Press, 1983.

Nicol, Adelheid A.M. and PennyM. Pexman. *Presenting Your Findings: A Practical Guide for Creating Tables.* Washington, DC: American Psychological Association, 1999.

Neuman, W. Lawrence. *Social Research Methods: Qualitative and Quantitative Approaches.* Fourth Edition. Boston: Allyn & Bacon, 2000.

Organization for Economic Co-operation and Development. *Promoting Research Excellence: Approaches to Funding.* Paris: OECD, 2014.

Page, Ruth, David Barton, Johann W. Unger and Michele Zappavigna. *Researching Language and Social Media: A Student Guide.* London: Rutledge, 2014.

Panneerselvam, R. *Research Methodology.* Second Edition. Delhi: PHI Learning Private Limited, 2012.

Patton, Michael .Quinn. *Qualitative Research and Evaluation Methods.* Third edition. Thousand Oaks, California: Sage, 2002.

Pecorari, Diane. *Academic Writing and Plagiarism: A Linguistic Analysis.* New York, New York.: Continnuum, 2008.

Peterson, Robert A. *Constructing effective Questionnaires.* Thousand Oaks, California: Sage, 2000.

Punch, Keith F. and Alis Quncea, *Introduction to Research Methods in Education.* Second Edition. Washington, DC: Sage, 2014.

Pyrczak, Fred and Randall R. Bruce. *Writing Empirical Research Reports: A Basic Guides for Students of the Social and Behavioral Sciences.* Fifth Edition. Glendale, California: Pyrczak, 2005.

Richards, Janet C and Miller, Sharon K. *Doing Academic Writing in Education: Connecting the Personal and the Professional.* Mahwah, New Jersey: Lawrence Erlbaum Associates, 2005.

Rubin, Herbert J. and Irene S. Rubin. *Qualitative Interviewing: The Art of Hearing Data.* Thousand Oaks, California.: Sage, 1995.

Saldanha, Gabriela and Sharon O'Brien. *Research Methodologies in Translation Studies.* New York, New York: Routledge, 2013.

Scott, Creg & Roberta Garner, *Doing Qualitative Research: Designs, Methods, and Techniques,* First Edition. Upper Saddle River, New Jersey: Pearson, 2013.

Silverman, David. *Doing Qualitative Research.* Fourth Edition. London: Sage, 2013.

Strauss, Anselm L. *Qualitative Analysis for Social Scientists.* Cambridge: Cambridge University Press, 1987.

Suter, W. Newton. *Introduction to Educational Research: A Critical Thinking Approach.* Thousand Oaks, California: Sage, 2005.

Swales, John and Christine B. Feak. *Academic Writing for Graduate Students: Essential Tasks and Skills.* Second Edition. Ann Arbor, Michigan: The University of Michigan Press, 2004.

Swanborn, Peter, *Case Study Research: What, Why and How.* Thousand Oaks, California: Sage, 2010.

Taylor, Bill, Gautam Sinha and Taposh Ghoshal. *Research Methodology: A Guide for Researchers in Management and Social Sciences.* New Delhi: PHI Learning Private Limited, 2006.

Tomal, Daniel R. *Action Research for Educators.* Second Edition. Rowman & Littlefield, 2010.

Upgade, Vijay and Arvind Shede. *Research Methodology.* Second Edition. New Delhi: S. Chand and Company Ltd, 2012.

Vyhmeister, Nancy Jean. *Quality Research Papers: For Students of Religion and Theology.* Second Edition. Grand Rapids, Michigan: Zondervan, 2008.

Yin, Robert K. *Case Study Research: Designs and Methods.* Third Edition. Thousand Oaks, California: Sage, 2003.

White Patrick. *Developing Research Questions: A Guide for Social Scientists.* Basingstoke: Palgrave Macmillan, 2009.

Wood, Peter. *Successful Writing for Qualitative Researchers.* London: Routledge, 1999.

Index of Names

Index of Subjects

CPSIA information can be obtained
at www.ICGtesting.com
Printed in the USA
LVHW031502120919
630869LV00012B/1048